Photo By Scott Blatt

Printed in the United States of America

First Printing, 2020

ISBN - 9798656200271

Graphic Design: Creative Image Design Group, Moorpark, California

Special gratitude: Curtis Dahl Photography

Sunrise and Roots

A Transcontinental Life

Diana Addison Lyle

FOREWARD

Several years ago, a brush fire was blazing on the hills behind our house. The fire department contacted us and reassured us the fire had taken another direction away from our neighborhood. So at 10:00 p.m. we put our little boy to bed, and retired for a much-needed good night's rest.

At 4:00 a.m. we received an emergency phone call telling us that the fire had switched directions and that we had to evacuate immediately. Shortly afterwards, our doorbell rang, and to my surprise when I opened the door, there stood Di Lyle, ready to help. That's the kind of person this lady is. As you read this incredible book, you'll discover the many roads that she has traveled.

Di doesn't do anything halfway. She has the ability to take both the good and the bad in life, and turn it into something special. After reading her book, I fully understood why at 4:00 in the morning in the middle of a fire, she showed up to help my family.

I'm honored to have her as my friend, and I truly believe she is one of a kind.

Bob Eubanks

Hwange Bull Elephant

CHAPTER 1

Hwange

You know you are truly alive when you're living among lions
- Isak Dinesen, Out of Africa

I grew up in Africa. It was a place where the rich red soil promised fertility and life. Our luxuriantly nutritious bedrock worked harmoniously with the omnipotent sun – giving birth to vegetation so green that it must have set new chlorophyll records. Rain showers came in the appropriate quantities, and monkeys came out to play on wet tree branches as soon as the white clouds squeezed out their last water droplet for the day.

Our haven was the highlands of Zimbabwe in Africa's southern hemisphere. Our home was perched at an altitude of 4,865 feet above sea level and 1,313 miles from the equator. Just like the fairytale about Goldilocks and the Three Bears, it was never too hot, and never too cold. The sun shared appropriate amounts of heat with its friend, the rain clouds. The red earth pulsated with the birth of every organism vital to the ecosystem. The natural food chain operated harmoniously, mostly devoid of unnecessary suffering.

Our childhood summers exploded with vitality. Early mornings were intoxicatingly inviting. We willed ourselves out of our crisp cotton-sheeted beds to run outside barefooted. That early-morning ritual of bouncing our lithe bodies across warm, dew-soaked grass invoked an inexorable pleasure that we shared with our dogs. As our four-legged friends gamboled after us, tongues hanging loosely out of their mouths to reduce the heat-generated temperatures, we celebrated each sizzling moment of this child dog union. While they drooled delicious doses of saliva, we laughed unrestrainedly. As the morning progressed and the sun's rays pointed more directly, more insistently upon the cracking lines of the red earth, we would run back to the shelter of the house with flush-faced satisfaction.

The African trees that became a visceral part of my early childhood soul were the msasa and baobab trees. The msasa captivated me for distinctive reasons: known also as the zebrawood, its shape made perfect sense. This medium-sized tree with rich wine-colored blooms has a broad canopy at its highest point that provides an umbrella-like shelter to people and animals that are over-heating. Its sensibility seared upon me an early understanding of the perfection of nature – how one living thing depends upon another. In later years, whenever I flew into Zimbabwe, and our airplane descended below the cloud line, I'd find the familiar tops of the msasa trees from my sky perch, and know that I was home. It invoked a deeply comforting feeling.

Baobab trees seeped into my soul for different reasons. They proliferate in the lower regions of Africa and can live to 3,000 years. Their enormous size creates the growth of massive trunks that are conveniently hollow, allowing many creatures to adopt the tree as their secure home. Along Zimbabwe's Zambezi and Limpopo Rivers, it is believed that women living in kraals where baobabs are plentiful have more children than those living outside baobab zones. Scientists have proven that it is likely due to the fact that they consume soup made from baobab leaves, which is rich in vitamins, creating a much higher fertility rate.

In my younger years, I admit to being wholly disinterested in that piece of science since I was sure that babies came from storks. I was far more drawn to the associative value that baobabs held for me. Our family's annual vacations were always to Zimbabwe's then-famous game reserves. Given the widespread decimation in the previous one hundred years of Africa's wild animal population, Zimbabwe created sanctuary areas in which we could still, respectfully, visit the magnificent creatures that remained. My first vivid memory in my toddler years was of a massive baobab tree that was home to so many happy animals. Its image against an orange African sky represented something acutely special, something sacred. And that's where we were headed in this upcoming story. I was seven years old.

Our family car – a pale blue Zephyr – careened over corrugated dirt roads as my mother, brothers and I followed the signs to Hwange National Park (formerly known as Wankie). This was the first expedition that I recall vividly. We were traveling from our hometown of Harare to the great wilds of Africa in the northwestern region of Zimbabwe. My brother Anthony's distinguished position as oldest sibling allowed him the privilege of sitting next to our mother in the front seat. Without the security of seatbelts, Stephen and I jolted across the benched back seat of the car, holding in our breaths as heat-laden dust plumes pelted our faces through the car's open windows.

An air of foreboding soon interrupted our childlike anticipation. An army roadblock warded off our access to the great wild animal conservancy. Camouflaged soldiers wearing thick, heavy boots marched towards us. All I saw were their oversized boots looming before my eyes.

"Good afternoon madam," said the lead soldier. "What is the purpose of your travels?"

Mum smiled at the three soldiers disarmingly and annunciated her words carefully:

"I'm taking my children to see the wild animals. You see, my husband is away on business, and he will join the family later."

The lead soldier replied matter-of-factly, "We don't recommend that you travel in this area. There have been some incidents and we do not believe this to be a safe place at the present time."

A child's perception of the world is couched within limited time frames. As my seven-year-old brain listened to the soldier's words delivered politely and formally, I figured that "at the present time" meant that in twenty minutes' time, the danger would magically disappear, and all would be well with the world.

As the cat sunglasses my mother was wearing pointed towards the horizon, I knew she meant business as she pressed down the car's accelerator with renewed determination. "Off we go, children," she announced. "Mummy must drive fast now." Our musically gifted mother had deduced that a car full of children was significantly safer at James Bond driving speeds.

I wasn't exactly sure from whom we were fleeing. Perhaps it was from one of those huge, black-maned African lions that I so desperately wanted to see in person. Pictures no longer cut it for me; I wanted to see Mr. Lion as close as was safe to stalk him. I was confident in mum's protective faculties, and decided that either we would be fleeing from Mr. Lion or sneaking up on him without bothering him too much.

How wrong I was – on all counts. As we entered the electric-fenced sanctuary of Hwange National Park, I watched mum exhale with relief – as if she felt her brood were safe from the unpredictable world outside the gates. As she drove the Zephyr more slowly on bumpy roads straddled by long, dry grass, I watched as she lit up her umpteenth cigarette of the day, blowing twirls of white smoke away from her cat-shaped sunglasses. Mum always impressed upon us how socially acceptable it was to smoke cigarettes in the car, but never out of the car. That was déclassé. I figured that was because smoking outside the car would result in the grass catching fire. Sensible.

"Look children," she whispered, "look carefully through the grass. Can you see anything?"

We were so focused on what lay in the grass to the left and right of our car windows that we forgot to look ahead: there in front of us was a mightily determined bull elephant with the longest ivory tusks I had ever seen - heading right towards us with a set of gigantic ears at right angles to his body. Instead of flapping, his ears remained widely positioned, and then the next "oh no" movement followed: he began to shake his head furiously while continuing his crescendoing march towards our Zephyr.

At stage three of his warning signals, mum rammed the car into reverse gear, and began to drive backwards faster than I had ever imagined a car could move in that direction. As her neck spiraled between the danger in front and the plumes of dust behind us, Anthony, Stephen and I braced ourselves as mum ploughed the car over ant hills, acacia tree branches, and python holes. It was frighteningly exhilarating, the sort of action I'd seen in movies. Surely this was better than Tarzan and the Apes; better than Mowgli in the Jungle Book. Mum still had the cigarette slotted in her mouth, and only when the massive bull elephant gave up on us, did she remove the misshapen butt from her mouth. I couldn't wait to tell my friends at school how we had escaped an early death.

As we settled into our rustic stone-walled cottage at Hwange that night, my father arrived. I'm not sure if he arrived by helicopter or flying saucer, but he and mum vacated the premises to go off and enjoy a childfree, romantic dinner together. My brothers and I ensconced ourselves under our malarial mosquito protection nets, tired and ready to sleep after an action-packed day. The sleep part, however, became problematic. We were so wired and sensitized to more stimuli than we had ever experienced before that we began to ask each other life's complicated questions:

"Do you think the elephant meant to kill us?"

"Do you think a small mosquito knows how to crawl through this net?"

That part I could handle. The next part I couldn't. As the night wore on, the sounds of Africa began to permeate through the walls of our stone cottage. If you have never heard a lion roar in the African bush, it's a revelation of jaw-dropping magnitude. Far more than a loud, guttural growl, it's a vibrational awakening; a penetrating ground shake that affirms the lion's status in the kingdom. I held onto my pillow as if it were going to perform life-saving treatment. An anxious night ensued.

The sound of an African tribe nearby, who were celebrating Saturday evening under the stars, was my next clear memory of that night. Their drums began to beat at a reasonable pace but within an hour, the beats were amplified with urgent speed. Anthony crept out of the cottage door to perform a reconnaissance and report back.

"Yep," he said. "There are lots of people half naked and some have weird skins and things around their ankles."

Anthony's big brother responsibility role continued.

"Remember the soldier at the road block today? Some people got murdered. That's why the man was telling mum that it wasn't safe for us to be in the area."

This was sensory overload: first the lions roaring, then the tribal drums beating, and now I was being informed that we were in the midst of a killing field.

It was only years later that I learned that after Rhodesia (Zimbabwe's former name) declared independence from Great Britain in 1965, African liberation groups' peaceful methods of struggle against the oppressive white Rhodesian government proved futile, so they opted to operate as underground movements, infiltrating back into Rhodesia as armed liberation fighters from the bases of Zambia and Tanzania, our northern neighbors. The second War of Liberation (Chimurenga II) began in earnest in April 1966 in the area surrounding our destination – Hwange National Park - and the battles intensified by 1968. The military skirmishes between the Rhodesian security forces and the Zimbabwean African National Union (ZANU) were as unpredictable as warfare is intended to be. The element of surprise was their strength, and the civilian casualties and the death toll mounted as quickly as our childhood innocence evaporated.

Our weekend in Hwange National Park was the first clear recollection I have of the world being so incredibly beautiful while also being so dangerously imperfect. The juxtaposition of the immense beauty of baobab trees set against red night skies, tribal people celebrating full stomachs and story-telling under a star-lit sky, magnificent elephants defending their territory, majestic lions reveling in their strength with prideful voices – was tempered by my new-found knowledge that there was something seriously wrong in paradise.

Diana, Anthony and Stephen

Anthony, Madam, Di 1968

Prime Minister Ian Douglas Smith declaring Rhodesia's Unilateral Independence from Britain

Joshua Nkomo, leader of one of the Zimbabwean liberation groups during the War

Mum with Dad's German friends about to fly into Victoria Falls, Zimbabwe

CHAPTER 2

Highlands

Moon river, wider than a mile, I'm crossing you in style some day
- Breakfast at Tiffany's

Our mother, Lily Overend Addison, was a woman worthy of her own trilogy. She was musically gifted, accomplished, single-mindedly determined, glamorous, generous, and volatile. When she was swept up by life's infinite possibilities, she was a creative force of inestimable proportions.

My cat-sunglassed mother with the tiny waist was undeterred by Zimbabwean army blockades. Her will always generated a way. Despite the imminent and present danger of military activity in the Hwange National Park area, nothing could dissuade her from accomplishing her goals.

"We are going to see the wild animals, children – swiftly so!"

It was as if she felt the elephants or the lions must save us from the obstacle: the part about a real war that she couldn't quite reconcile within her imaginative picture. The Hwange weekend was a demarcation line in our childhoods. At least it was for me.

A few weeks after returning to our home in Harare, mum and dad announced that they were heading off to the Victoria Falls, one of the seven greatest natural wonders of the world. Its beauty and attraction were undeniable. The only problem with the choice is that it was on the border of Zambia, and courtesy of Anthony, I was now fully informed of the military insurgency spilling over the Zimbabwean Zambian border.

As befitted mum, she looked absolutely ravishing when she bade us farewell. This time her cat sunglasses were paired with snappy leggings that accentuated her slender legs, and a perfectly ironed cream blouse was tucked into her waist. A headscarf came along for the ride in case of any high-flying action.

"Bye, bye children," she called out to us as she drove away in the car with dad.

"Listen to nanny, and we'll bring you back something nice from the Falls."

Three days later, mum and dad returned home with contorted shoulders and pallid exhaustion written all over their faces. As promised, they brought us little gifts. Mine was a six-inch-tall angry-faced hairy baboon that slept with me in my bed for a full year. As they relayed the details of their disastrous weekend to us, I concluded that mum's headscarf must have been really useful during their high-flying action. It turned out that it was the low-flying action that became inextricably more dangerous.

Mum always swapped out her Peter Stuyvesant cigarettes for her much stronger Russian Sobranie cigarettes when her nerves were shot. I recognized that this story was in a new phase of severity as she lit up a strong Sobranie. In between inhalations, she described the drama they experienced at Victoria Falls with punctuated exhalations:

"We got into the small plane with our German visitors, and as we were flying over the Falls, one of them kept requesting that the pilot go 'lower'. The pilot followed the orders and the plane started flying under the lip of the waterfall inside the spray area. We were right inside the Victoria Falls and couldn't see a thing because we were drenched in thousands of gallons of water!"

Mum always disowned her association with anyone she deemed to be selfishly cavalier. Once they had lost her trust, they were no longer hers and dad's friends. They were only 'his friends'.

She continued, "as if that wasn't dangerous enough, dad's friend kept shouting to the pilot, 'down...go lower, go lower'. It was terrifying."

Miraculously, the plane didn't plummet into the Victoria Falls and everyone survived to tell the story.

I always imagined that the equator was some kind of deep dark hole into which people and animals fell and disappeared. The risk standard for our lives seemed to be edging closer in latitude towards the equator, although it probably wasn't any different from previous years. I was just more aware of it.

Though the circumference of our family vacations narrowed down to places closer to home, there was always some adrenalin spiking action in our weekly lives. Mum sped through life with fantastical dreams that showcased themselves in so many indelible and beautiful ways.

Mum and dad's Saturday night dinner parties in Harare were legendary in the social circles of our northern suburbs. We had a modest house in

Highlands, but mum always pulled out a culinary coup de grâce. She and her sisters grew up intercontinentally, and all five sisters cultivated the art of mastering the most flavorful creations of the most delectable dishes from across the world. Their cooking expertise was in a rare league. French, Italian and Middle Eastern dishes were enhanced, crossbred and artfully upgraded.

Once a month, mum would transform our home into a movie set from a make-belief world. Dad was her co-producer, and he contributed his own accouterments – a set of technological skills that were way ahead of his time. While mum headed up the kitchen staff three days in advance, I watched dad set up movie projectors, speakers and wired-up contraptions.

As Saturday arrived, Bonnet, our faithful, loyal and hard-working cook, was on never-ending duty, following mum's instructions assiduously. Sometimes, when mum was between languages in her distracted excitement, she'd refer to Bonnet as Chapeau (in French), and he'd smile at her – looking confused. I watched through the kitchen window as the cooking flavors and smells began to permeate through the house. The aromas spoke to my taste buds and they began exploding in anticipation of the night's bounty.

Watching mum in her bedroom dressing up for the occasion held its own voyeuristic pleasure. She always wore sensuously long dresses and enlisted my tuxedo-dressed dad in the ritualistic zipping-up-the-dress process. Her dresses were ethereal, sumptuous. As mum became an increasingly more remote and inaccessible figure, the dresses she wore were a visual reminder of her performance presence - and I was somewhere up a tree, entranced by what I saw, but ultimately a member of a quite different species.

By nightfall, the dogs were ushered into our bedroom for safety, along with Anthony, Stephen and I who were barred from any kind of appearance. With the animals safely intact with us (although heaven only knew where the Siamese cats were), the gates were opened to welcome the stream of cars arriving at our portal. Dad had already tarmacked our driveway at the onset of the dinner party season so that all the guests' dinner attire would remain impeccably clean – devoid of grass stains or high heels sinking into red earth.

The scene was everything I hoped adulthood would look like for me once my body complied and fast-tracked me to that grownup phase. My brothers and I slid like reptiles on our stomachs to dad's study so that we could peek at the exotic scene from windowsill level. Handsome, dapper men opened car doors to tall, slender women who unfurled themselves gracefully out of their sunken car seats. Their hair was teased enough to give them an extra three inches in height, and the jewels that hung from their ear-lobes glittered enticingly.

I shall always remember the pure Hollywood glamor that exuded from Thelma Landau. She wore a long pink gown over her summer-tanned skin. Her blonde hair was swept up regally, and her wide shoulders were figuratively important: they represented a new breed of women in Africa; women who were strong, capable and not as dependent on men as frightened me.

Then there was Peggy Henderson, the elegant, long-suffering wife of Ian Henderson, the pompous alcoholic. She arrived bracing herself for a night in which her husband would end up maudlin drunk, hitting on all the other women. Her favorite contemporary song of the time was *Long legged Woman Dressed in Black,* and I always wanted to re-write her anthem to read, 'Long legged Woman Fraught with Bad Luck'.

The dinner commenced with music that transported my ears to the south of France. *Breakfast at Tiffany's* and Henry Mancini's *Moon River* was my absolute favorite sound, although I'm not quite sure how my map dart arrived geographically at the south of France because *Breakfast at Tiffany's* was in New York. *Lara's Theme* from *Doctor Zhivago* was another musical highlight of the evening, and because Omar Sharif starred in that, and he was Egyptian by nationality, I had no trouble transporting myself to North Africa, the land of his birth. Since my mum's family spent a lot of time in Alexandria, Egypt, and supposedly, my grandfather played bridge with Omar Sharif, I almost felt like the movie star was part of our family.

As dad performed his touch as the cinematic sound technician of mum's culinary masterpiece evening, my brothers and I once again slithered on our reptilian stomachs, this time like lizards darting our tongues out in anticipation of a feast. The kitchen counters were loaded with enough food for another three dinner parties, and as Bonnet packed the left-over dishes into the refrigerator, we intercepted him with Oliver-type bowls and pleas. Since the ever-patient Bonnet was fully accustomed to our after-dinner ritual, he smiled caringly as he heaped our plates full of wine-drenched filet mignon, sweet glazed carrots, baby potatoes extraordinaire, and our favorite cauliflower cheese. We were careful to leave room in our stomachs for dessert. Chocolate mousse with peppermint chips was our favorite, as was mum's Spanish crème and endless choices of labor-intensive French pastries.

Replete with bulging stomachs and satisfied palates, we completed our participation of the evening's third act by planting ourselves beneath one of the bedroom windows where we had a night owl's view of the men on the front lawn - drinking brandy and smoking cigars. We covered both genders, moving stealthily to our parents' bedroom where we hid underneath the bed so that we could watch the ladies come in to powder their noses. We had to stifle our giggles as Claudia, Gloria and Peggy discussed the merits of having children.

For the most part, I very much respected my parents' choice in friends. They led lives of integrity and I recall the intelligent conversations they shared. My first strong role models came from this group, and as the political situation in Zimbabwe deteriorated, I recall admiring the difficult moral stances they made when they were so clearly going against the white minority status quo.

The best act of the dinner evening, the final act, was what I looked forward to the most. This time, my brothers and I stationed ourselves behind the dining room door and it was through that peephole that we could watch the débonnaire men hold onto the pretty women as they swished their dresses around the dance floor. There was such a graceful fluidity of movement as the Viennese waltz transitioned into the foxtrot and later, the tango, a dress rehearsal, perhaps, for some of the mind games that would cap off the night.

If Sir Victor Hugo and his glamorous wife with the long red nails, Lady Sebright, were able to attend mum's dinner parties, an extra layer of extravagant excitement was added to the memory bank film footage. Anthony had his eyes set on their daughter, Liza, and Victor would fly his small plane in from the Melsetter district in eastern Zimbabwe, and land it in Harare on makeshift runways. His eccentric outfits always delighted us. If Liza spent the night with us, there was a fourth dimension of limitless fun.

Our parents and their friends contributed more food towards actualizing our dreams than we recognized at the time. In Richard and Thelma Landau, we were given access to a part of Africa where running freely in the wilds expanded our imaginations limitlessly. In Bill and Avril Whitaker we acquired knowledge, sensibility and bravery. We learned that the right road, the humane road, was not always the easy road. In Diana Mcoran Campbell, we learned positivity and fortitude. There were so many invaluable gifts we were given as children during these dreamful African nights.

Di, Steve, Anthony, James. Highlands, Zimbabwe 1969

Diana McOran Campbell at Mum's dinner parties

Eileen, Mum, Claudia - Dinner Party 1975

Diana, Mum, Dad, Stephen, Anthony - Poolside, Highlands, Harare

Steve, Di and Anthony - Harare

CHAPTER 3

Beira

The Earth was made round so that we would not see too far down the road
- Isak Dinesen, Out of Africa

I f the northern section of Zimbabwe bordering Zambia had become too much of a military hot bed, Lily Addison found a palliative alternative for our family vacations. Despite the much-publicized fact that in 1964, our eastern neighbor, Mozambique, had started its own war of liberation against its Portuguese colonialists, mum calculated that the anti-colonial political group, Front for the Liberation of Mozambique (FRELIMO), was not gaining enough military traction against the Portuguese regular army to give rise to any safety concerns.

"I think it's perfectly safe for us to take a lovely vacation to the Mozambique coast. They're not shooting anyone on the beaches."

I often wonder whether my innate aversion to the Indian Ocean began with that fateful trip. To this day, I view the Indian Ocean as this inky dark-blue, blackish vortex of impending doom. Whenever I hear about the latest pirate attack on ships, it's always in the dreaded Indian Ocean. Admittedly, the attacks are usually off the coast of Somalia, but the math shows me that Somalia is only 1797 miles from Mozambique, and that qualifies it as pirate-operational territory.

Our worn-out, pale blue Zephyr was in for the worst trip of its mechanical life. This time, our whole family descended upon its chassis, including Dochas, our much-loved childhood nanny. Since this was a weeklong trip, we had substantially more luggage. Mum's packing list included several colorful evening outfits for the promisingly sophisticated nights out in the Portuguese-colonized coastal town of Beira.

By 1969, four years into Zimbabwe's (Rhodesia at the time) Unilateral Declaration of Independence from the world, our edible world became pedestrian. Courtesy of our nutritious African soil, we grew all our own organic vegetables and shared the smorgasbord with the natural creatures that feasted on our produce. But mum grew tired of spinach, pumpkin, beans and tomatoes. Her culinary creative flair was being stifled. With widespread shortages of food products that we no longer imported into our sanctioned, landlocked country, mum yearned for the exotic delicacies that came from the sea: mussels, oysters, lobster tails, caviar.

As mum packed for our Beira trip, she literally chose outfits from her closet that would pair well with her mussel evening out on the town; the yellow caftan was for her crab evening expedition; the green cocktail dress for the lobster fiesta. Since this trip was anticipated with such huge expectations, mum ditched the cat sunglasses and donned her Lauren Bacall oversized pair.

We waved goodbye to our gardener, who was charged with taking care of our dogs, cats, tortoises and rabbits. The sunken-down Zephyr struggled to gear itself up to any reasonable speed, and as we crawled out of the city into the countryside, I had little hope that we'd reach Beira before my old age.

As we crossed the border into Mozambique, I watched a visible rejuvenation in mum take place. At long last, she could utilize her multi-lingual capabilities and marinade her multi-cultural roots in the flavors of Portugal. With her Lauren Bacall glasses propped sportingly on her head, she began her discourse with the customs official in Portuguese.

"Se você por favor," she asked.

"Posso ver seus passaportes", the official requested.

"Obrigado," she called out, when he handed back our papers to her without incident.

Dad was particularly good about standing aside and supporting mum when he saw her escape the claustrophobia of living in a sanctioned, isolated country. She yearned for intercontinental connection, language gymnastics. Our trip to Beira was her springtime and Lily's new shoots came out to play.

The only problem was that it was the height of summer, and maybe that was a forewarning of a pot that was about to boil over. Our highlands home in Harare gave us the world's best climate. Just like Goldilocks and the Three Bears, it was never too hot, and never too cold. Nobody prepared us for a 100-degree-fahrenheit journey in the back of a searingly hot, sluggish car with Dochus, Anthony, Stephen and I trapped for fourteen hours. Our Disneyland expectations of the trip rapidly vaporized with the rising heat from the burning tarmac. Mum's packed pasties and sausage rolls lost their allure. Anthony hung his legs and feet out of the window in an attempt to cool off but he complained that the hot wind was grazing his skin.

During the interminably long fourteen hours, we dozed off in disappointment. Perhaps that was the initial dampener that set the ill-fated Beira trip off course. We had never experienced humidity at this level. It was suffocating, oppressive, and the unbreathable globules of dirty, hot molecules seemed to weigh down our legs and our spirits. As we pulled into Beira, and dad parked in front of the ocean, he encouraged us to stretch our legs and run towards the water. We squinted at him as if he had lost all his common senses. Why would anybody want to run in this heat? Why move?

I recall so vividly my first sight of the Indian Ocean. The saturated humidity had created a dark gray cloud layer over the water. Since it's known to be a particularly deep ocean, it relies on the blue sky to lighten its morbid appearance. Not on this day. The water was churned up with muddy dirt from all the rivers that had flowed into it recently, and it didn't look anything like the tropical oasis I had seen in pictures. All I wanted to do was go home – back to our better paradise in Zimbabwe with its blue skies punctuated by happy white puffs of clouds.

As we unpacked in an apartment one street removed from the oceanfront, I recoiled into the children's room with Dochus, and asked her if she could sleep with me that night. She and I seemed to understand the trashing of life's dreams. Her dreams were trashed long before I met her. Perhaps when we awoke in the morning, Beira would have undergone a metamorphosis – an overnight betterment project with a more attractive tomorrow.

The next morning, Anthony, Stephen and I ventured out with hopeful hearts, determined to direct the outcome of the day with our unbridled enthusiasm. As we meandered down the street, our leader, Anthony, pointed towards a young boy who had a Vervet monkey on a long, heavy chain. This was like manna from heaven. I had always loved monkeys and felt a particular affinity to them because I was born with monkey arms: long, thin, pliable, quick-reflexed monkey arms that served me well when I wrestled my brothers to the floor.

My monkey arms were enormously useful, too, when I climbed up our avocado tree to access our home-built tree house. Afternoons in that tree house were particularly special when our summer rain showers came pouring down. I'd remain inside the wooden shelter until the rain abated – waiting for the treat of all treats: as soon as the rain subsided, and the sun came out, all the African creatures would come out, singing and playing in celebration. White-faced Vervet monkeys did a lot of loving after African rain showers, and we'd always call it 'a monkey's wedding', because that was the respectable Catholic answer to some really weird physical antics. How fortuitous it was that my favorite African monkey was waiting to welcome me on this meltingly hot day in Beira. Victory came in cute packages.

The first obstacle was language. The monkey's owner couldn't speak English and unlike our mother, we could not speak Portuguese. All I had picked up from mum's interactions were "if you please" in Portuguese. So we resorted to sign language and arm gestures. The Vervet monkey honed in on Anthony and I, tilting its head curiously as he sized up our intentions. We responded enthusiastically as we approached what we thought was an afternoon of ground-breaking scientific discovery: the monkey's ability to interact with Anthony and Diana.

"Mr. Monkey. Would you like to shake our hand?"

"Never mind. Would you like a banana?"

How naïve we were. A giant moth flew past the monkey's head, and he used his fast reflexes to grab it out of the air and settle it into his hands for wing dismantling. I began to express my awe at the monkey's dexterous speed by giggling, and just then, he stared at Anthony and I with a plan in his head. Within seconds, while still holding onto the giant moth, he jumped about six feet onto Anthony's shoulder, and sunk his front teeth into his neck. Before I even had time to respond to the shock, the monkey jumped from Anthony's shoulder onto my bare thigh, and sunk his teeth deeply into the top part of my tanned leg.

I always took my direction from Anthony. He determined that it probably wasn't a good idea to hang out with the monkey any more, and so we said goodbye politely to the Portuguese boy, who didn't seem to think it was a big deal that his pet monkey just bit two strangers and left a trail of blood as evidence.

That was my first early lesson into how wrong and cruel it is to turn wild animals into pets. The idea that they are blissfully happy being fed by us could not be further from the truth. This was a frustrated, angry Vervet monkey who lashed out at us unpredictably because he was chained to a heavy piece of metal – away from the significant bonds that monkeys need with their troop families. This was not his fault but rather our baptism into human idiocy.

The next part of this story is the one – looking back – that I still can't quite comprehend. As Anthony and I bled profusely, we decided that we had to find the closest public bathroom to blot up the blood with bathroom tissue. Our first instinct was not to run back to the apartment to seek help from our parents. We were afraid of our mum's reaction to all the blood; that she would ask us what we'd done. Maybe we weren't supposed to be around someone's pet monkey. Maybe this was our fault, and she'd be furious with us.

We conjured up a bizarre plan to hide the evidence of there ever having been a monkey or two serious monkey bites. Somehow we'd enlist Stephen to creep back into our holiday apartment, go into our luggage, and ferret out some sweaters or scarves that we could wrap around Anthony's neck and my leg. And that's precisely what we did.

That evening, as we seated ourselves at the dining room table, Anthony wrapped a yellow sweater around his neck. He was lucky to have one since we'd mostly only packed summer clothing. I wrapped some t-shirts around my leg, and we both put on an Oscar-worthy performance at the table - feigning absolute normality. But warm, liquid blood that won't clot is persistent in its tracks. As Anthony sat at dinner, mum noticed that there was red blood seeping determinedly through his sweater-wrapped neck. The yellow sweater betrayed our secret!

Mum and dad whisked us off to a local hospital with herculean speed, and within minutes we had needles punched into our arms, transporting the rabies vaccine. I don't recall Anthony and I ever telling mum what bit us, but she clearly recognized what looked like animal bite marks, and rabies shots were the standard response to that.

Our January 1970 Beira vacation had disastrous omens inscribed all over it. That night, as we tried to fall asleep, we were awoken to mum screaming at dad in a midnight fight. I don't know if adults fully realize the effect that their angry outbursts have on very young children. It terrified us and gave us the sense that the world was falling off its axis. Even more concerning was Anthony's response to it.

I always knew my older brother to be highly intelligent. He took responsibility for Stephen and I at an early age and was brave, bold, adventurous and quick to make acutely logical decisions. The fault lines in his brain began to crack that night in Beira. Looking back, I so wish that I could have understood him better at age eight. My assertive, mature-beyond-his-years brother confronted mum the following morning with defiantly folded arms and burgeoning anger. He berated her for shouting at dad unrelentingly.

I will never know whether it was our monkey bites that caused our parents' fight that awful night. We were wrong in not going straight to them, but as is the case with most innocent children, we had our fears, and those fears told us to pretend that nothing ever happened. We hoped that it could all be magically erased.

The story didn't end well. A week later, when we were back in Zimbabwe, in Goldilocks and the Three Bears land, my leg turned septic with a bacterial infection. I recall lying in our white bath and seeing it looking swollen, purple and angry. Dr. Cantor was summoned to our house where I was feverish and very ill. To this day I do not know what the diagnosis was. Clearly the boy in Mozambique did not brush his pet monkey's teeth with Colgate toothpaste, and something rather nasty penetrated my blood stream.

That same week, our gentle nanny Dochus disappeared from our lives. I don't know whether she was let go or whether she went away on her own volition. All that mattered was that I was devastated at the loss of the only truly comforting maternal figure I had ever known. Dochus combed my hair in the mornings. She sat with me on the grass every afternoon and taught me how to make birds' nests out of tall, dry grass. We made intricately beautiful nests that could rival the artwork of Weaver birds. We'd sink our pudgy hands into sections of our garden where she determined there was more clay-like soil. Together we'd fashion the most beautiful pottery. Only someone who is inextricably tied to the land has that kind of innate knowledge. Dochus contributed so many vitally nourishing components to my life and I loved her deeply.

The Beira trip felt like a category four hurricane that battered our entire family almost irreparably. And then....along came hope.

Vervet Monkey that bit Anthony and Di in Beira

Mum and Thelma Landau

Laura and Richard Landau

CHAPTER 4

Umwinsidale

This place you are going to - you must make a very big fire so I can find you
- Out of Africa

The restorative power of fresh starts was impressed upon me at age eight. The ingrained sadness my brothers and I experienced after losing our caring nanny, Dochus, the strong matriarchal presence in our lives, was palpable after Beira. People can never be replaced but regeneratively hopeful phases in our lives repair us.

We met the Landau family. Richard and Thelma Landau had three children and their son, Paddy, enlisted piano lessons with our mother. Thelma and mum cemented an immediate bond while dad and Richard found a solid connection indulging their verbal acuity and dry senses of humor.

Laura Landau was a few years younger than me and I rejoiced at the opportunity this presented: at last I could have a baby sister; a scrunchable, adorable baby sister with blonde curls. When I discovered that this new little sister didn't have toddler temper tantrums, I calculated the bonus score on that. It was like a triple hand of kings in cards.

As our friendship flourished through the years, we grew to relish the car rides between Harare and the Landau's home twenty miles north of the city. We'd always stop off at Bon Marché, Richard's successful business, to load up on delicious delicacies. Once that was accomplished, Laura and I would race to the third back seat of the station wagon. Children usually don't do that; they're more likely to be avidly jockeying for the front seat so that they can feel more grown-up, more adult-like. Not us. The third back seat's positioning held a particular attraction because it faced the traffic behind us, so this was an amusing opportunity to spread a lot of love in the world by waving at all the strangers.

The highlight of the ride was when Thelma played *Peter and the Wolf* on the car's sound system. I'd ignite Laura's imagination by making hand gestures timed to the music, and her responses assured me of the emergence of a particularly special childhood chapter. Thelma would call out to Laura from the driver's seat,

"Who's my turtle dove?" and Laura would reply, "Lau-RA". It was precious in its purity.

The Landau family's home in a wild, rural area of Zimbabwe entrenched for me what I already knew: that the African bush was essential to my soul's peace. I wanted no part of city life with its noise, traffic, concrete and pollution. Our suburban home was a tolerable compromise until I discovered the Landau's Umwinsidale Eden. It had large stretches of open savanna with cascading waterfalls and large granite rocks for climbing and bringing out our inner monkey. The land's importance to me was solidified by the abundance of my favorite trees – the mystical msasas. Under their protective umbrellas, all living creatures could shelter and find rest – away from the dehydrating effect of the midday sun.

Umwinsidale was a utopian place that provided inexhaustible exploration possibilities. Long summer days turned into golden nights as we ran across acres of manicured lawns, up onto frangipani-bordered wooden bridges and around koi-filled ponds. Tairos and Carla, the family's two massive Great Danes, galloped after us excitedly. Even more unintendedly thrilling - Carla produced a surprise liter of thirteen Great Dane puppies. Laura and I ditched our dolls permanently and took up full-time caregiving duties inside the puppy nursery. We watched the miracle of their eyes opening after ten days, and helped Carla with her exhaustive feeding duties by bringing in extra bottles of puppy nourishment. I can remember so clearly the milky-breathed puppy smell permeating our senses remedially.

Every night, Laura and I would go to bed in a ship-cabin-inspired bedroom where we'd take turns heaving our little bodies up to the top bunk bed while one of us would stay below deck to take up the bow position. Once we were tucked in under the blankets, we'd fight encroaching sleep so that we could share our stories, but as our speech slurred, it was obvious that our eyelids were begging us to shut down. Our goodnight lullaby was always the sound of African grass owls hooting from the msasa treetops.

As soon as the sun peeped up from behind the hills in the morning, Laura and I bounced out of bed and sped like racing cheetahs to the sunroom, eagerly awaiting cook Bernie's hot, scrumptious breakfast. It didn't matter what was on the menu. Anything that Bernie served was sure to be a taste bud extravaganza. Even the freshly squeezed orange juice that we gulped down came from the world's sweetest oranges.

The pièce de résistance – the reason that waking up early was so vital - lay in the place we were about to visit. Laura and I couldn't skid out of the house fast enough to disappear a half mile down the road into long grass and brambles. The nettles that scratched our bare legs were a small price to pay for the oasis we were about to encounter: the Umwinsidale waterfall with its crystal clear, glinting water flowing across spectacular rock formations. If ever there was a perfect landscape, this was it. Laura and I were prepared to risk more than we envisaged as we made our weekly pilgrim's journey to the waterfall. On this particular day, however, we were forced to measure the potential cost.

After scouting the logistics, I came up with this plan:

"I don't think we can get to the lip of the waterfall because the water level has risen with the rain. We'll have to slither underneath those rocks."

Laura followed compliantly. As we crawled on our stomachs underneath the large, concave granite rock, a deadly force of nature confronted us. It was the forked tongue of one of Africa's deadliest snakes – the black mamba. A bite from one of these lethal serpents would render one of us dead within twenty minutes.

"Laurs," I whispered. "Back up!"

Our survival instincts turned us into lizard statues as we mastered the art of reverse crawling with barely any movement. It was a human feat of impossible proportions, one that we've never replicated again.

As we pulled ourselves upright, our brains tried to measure what we had just eluded. As the shock subsided, and the color returned to our cheeks, we started laughing uncontrollably. It was obvious what we had just escaped. I can't remember if, after our mamba meeting, we took a snakebite serum kit with us to future waterfall visits. What I do know for sure is that Anthony, Paddy, Stephen and Simon came with us more regularly from that time forward. The day's reckonings made us wiser as we formulated our future plan: there was safety in numbers.

We returned to the surety of home base that day where we were welcomed by Daffy the goat, who cut loose and was chewing on Thelma's tablecloth in the front garden; and for two, young snake-sobered girls there were rabbits and tortoises to feed. The Landau's backyard held a huge, protective enclosure in which rabbit warrens fed into the ground. Circled around this huge enclosure was Simon Landau's racecar track. He'd drive his miniature racecar around the oval driveway, displaying his quick reflexes at an early age. I'm not sure how the tortoises and rabbits felt about this piece of urban encroachment, but the rabbits' proliferating numbers indicated that it probably didn't bother them enough to stop breeding. Laura and I experienced yet another dimension of girlhood joy watching all the baby bunnies hip-hopping around – safe from predators.

Lydia Kafulani, the Landau's housekeeper, filled the incalculable void that Dochus' departure left. This generous-hearted young woman was selfless, gentle, nurturing, and filled with everything that I knew to be good.

When any one of us grazed our knees and came limping into the house dripping blood, Lydia was there. When we ran around the swimming pool area, and accidentally stepped on the long thorns that were a part of the vegetation, Lydia was there. When we stayed out in the sun too long and complained that evening of burning skin while watching *Spiderman* on TV, Lydia was there. When aggressive bees stung us, we'd yell "L-Y-D-I-A". Her tender arms gave us comfort. Her eyes assured us that we were loved.

When I returned to Zimbabwe in 2013, after not seeing Lydia for over thirty years, I tracked her down with Laura's help. As I drove up the driveway to her home, this beautiful woman who was then well into her seventies, ran towards the car as if she were still twenty. Her greeting enveloped my senses in an explicably powerful way. We embraced, and the same warmth and feelings of tenderness I'd felt as a child came rushing back tenfold. Lydia was not able to speak at first. Our emotions were still drinking in the moment; still absorbing the reality of our physical presences with eyes that spoke the thousand words that didn't need verbalization. When the time felt right, we wept tears of joy within the context of our shared humanity.

Lydia and I held each other's hands gently as we sat down to recount life's joys and blows the previous thirty years. Our farewell moment later on is seared comfortingly in my heart. Both of us sobbed, and as I drove the car away, Lydia ran after the car, and as I watched her in the rear view mirror still waving at my car until it disappeared over the horizon, the tears that streamed down my face were an enriching liquid assurance of the presence of one of life's most precious angels.

Di, Richard Landau, Jill - Cape Town 2014

Stephen, Anthony, Diana at Lake Chivero

Wildebeest crossing the Mara River - Photography by Scott Blatt.

CHAPTER 5

Lake Chivero and Fish Eagle's Nest

Summer will end soon enough, and childhood as well
- George R.R. Martin - A Game of Thrones

Our family mastered the art of dodging the war's more explosive areas by mapping out the benign zones for our family vacations. Lake Chivero (Lake McIllwaine at the time) was located just outside our hometown of Harare, which made it extra safe. It was a wild animal conservancy without Africa's 'big five' game – lion, leopard, elephant, rhinoceros and Cape buffalo – so we gave it a three out of five grading. Hwange (formerly known as Wankie), on the other hand, was our favorite wild animal stomping ground with a five out of five rating because of its wealth of scary, beautiful animals.

Anthony, Stephen and I were content with compromises.

"They can't have lions and leopards here," reasoned Anthony. "They'd kill all the people and farmers nearby if they did. Hwange is far away with much more space. Elephants need space so that's why they are at Hwange."

Lake Chivero still gave us the opportunity to see really cool-looking giraffe, zebra, eland – and our absolute favorite big antelope species – the glorious sable. These massive creatures had huge horns that curved backwards. With their striking black and white color, we found them captivating. We also loved to see large herds of impala all freeze while looking our way. Within seconds thereafter, they'd treat us to a graceful, structured run-for-their-lives exit that left us all gasping,

"Wow!"

There were two stonewalled cottages with thatched grass roofs at Lake

Chivero: Fish Eagle's Nest was at the top of the hill overlooking the lake. That was the prized positioning. The less fancy one was Mocking Chat Cottage – in the middle of the granite-stoned outcrop. It, too, was named after an African bird. We didn't care which one our parents chose. Each lodging gave us a back-to-nature adventure with protective malarial mosquito nets to sleep under at night. I loved the coziness of the white nets. As each of us climbed into bed we learned how to tuck them neatly under our mattresses – just like a silkworm's cocoon with a moth at the center. We'd lie awake - animatedly talking through the gauzy nets while our hissing paraffin lamps cast a shadowy glow in the room. The sound and smell of those paraffin lamps spelled exploration and exceptionally happy times. I loved sleeping in the same nest as my brothers.

As soon as the sun rose in the morning, Anthony, Stephen and I sneaked out of our cottage room without making a sound. Stone floors have many uses – not least of which is their soundproofing advantage. Each daylight second was filled with promising potential, and we planned to actively engage that potential.

"Shhhh. Don't wake mum and dad," we'd whisper to each other.

Within ten minutes of running away, the cottage was out of sight, and we were surrounded by dense vegetation. There should have been safety rules for visitors in the animal conservancy but we certainly hadn't read them. Anthony motioned to us to crouch in the grass. There was something there and we needed to be silent.

"It's something really big," Anthony mouthed to us. We were expert lip readers.

Just at that moment, the largest male kudu I had ever seen bounded out from behind a granite rock. His impressive, stately horns spoke of prominent strength as they curled their way up to the sky. We could feel the weight of his body through the vibrational thud of his hooves on the earth's surface. It was thrilling, and it made us want to penetrate the thicket more.

So we did. With a renewed sense of achievement, we felt like intrepid pioneers discovering the vast secrets of Africa's animal kingdom. It was much more exciting than driving in a car. Walking through the wild terrain gave us an insider's perspective; a close acquaintance with these mystical creatures. If anything chased us, we could run.

Our immaturity didn't factor in the characteristics of the African blue wildebeest – the muscular, front-heavy antelope with large horns shaped like a parenthesis. Every year in the Masai Mara National Reserve in Kenya, tens of thousands of wildebeest cross the Mara River in a mesmerizing formation. Their crossing is one of the last mass terrestrial wildlife movements left on the planet. The migration is also one of nature's great paradoxes because of the inherent danger involved in this massive crossing. Crocodiles are crafty creatures and they capitalize on this meal ticket by waiting underneath the water's surface. As the wildebeest cross the river, the crocodiles snatch them with their massively powerful jaws. I've been to the Masai Mara, witnessed this dramatic sight, and still view it as one of nature's cruelties. The wildebeests' movements are dictated by the arrival of the heavy rains, and they cross the Mara River when their instincts urge them to seek the most fertile grazing grounds on either side of the river.

On this day at Lake Chivero, there weren't any wildebeest crossings, but we were about to encounter a fairly large herd of these very wary animals. Anthony motioned for Stephen and I to follow him in careful-foot-placement single file. We obeyed each instruction. There, in front of us, were military rows of wildebeest staring at us intensely. They had already picked up our scent, and determined our presence long before we determined theirs. The peculiarity about wildebeest is that they are evasive creatures who have an inbuilt fear of us, but if cornered or startled, they become severely aggressive – particularly if they have babies in their midst. They will mock charge, show off their muscular abilities, and if necessary, actually charge. The herd we stumbled upon made it perfectly clear that they didn't like us, and the alpha male came forward and did an aggressive mock charge that made my brothers and I turn around – and run for our lives. In fact, that was a really stupid response on our part, because a wildebeest can outrun us easily. They're known to be able to reach speeds of fifty miles per hour when outrunning a chasing lion.

We ran through the brush, and then climbed up the hill. By the time we reached the safety of Fish Eagle's Nest, our hearts reminded us with their pounding beat that we'd just escaped another African risk. We loved it – became addicted to its adrenalin surge.

As the midday heat encroached, we copied the animals and sought the shade beneath the canopied trees. Mum and dad joined us for non-exertion board games. We played chess and draughts with competitive vigor. Anthony always beat us but that was because he was older. Age had huge advantages in childhood. On the rare occasion where I was able to take down Anthony's bishops or castles, I dramatically hit the pieces off the chessboard with a loud "Da-dum!" Once – only once – did I checkmate Anthony, and I shrieked the victory so loudly that it must have disturbed all the animals in the game reserve. I could vividly imagine Mrs. Giraffe saying wearily, "another crazy human."

Giraffe have become one of my all-time favorite animals. They have such gentle, large eyes with eyelashes that would make Kim Kardashian envious. When a giraffe runs across the African savannah, it is a sight of rare beauty. Their powerful, graceful motion is a mechanical work of art. Their spring-load capacity is incredible – a rhythmic example of supreme locomotive proficiency.

Later in the afternoons, mum and dad loaded us into the car for more animal sightings. It's a completely different experience from a car, but we were appreciative of any access we would gain to the great kingdom. When we returned back to Fish Eagle's Nest, we found evidence of the Vervet monkeys having tried every possible way to access the food in our cottage. There were sticky monkey paw prints all over our kitchen windows.

My brothers and I became avid animal-print experts. Like seasoned archaeologists, we'd stare at the rich African earth, and stop to analyze any tracking print that evoked extra special attention. Any signs that a print belonged to something big and dangerous - like a lion or leopard - made us stop in our tracks to perform a study. To this day, I am a semi expert on many African animals' tracking prints. I can tell most species by the print, the age of the print, and in what direction the animal is moving. It's an engrossing hobby that feeds my curiosity.

Lake Chivero was a special place in our childhoods. When Dean Wood's family parked their boat at the marina camping site across the lake, an extra dimension of excitement was added to our experience. The Woods' boat would blaze a trail across the water to our jetty where we were patiently waiting for our boat rides. I'm not sure how we knew what time they were coming, but somehow we were always at the jetty at the appropriate time. Dean took full control of the boat, being careful not to place his hands into the sides of the lake where the dreaded African disease, Bilharzia (snail fever), proliferated. If the parasitic Bilharzia worm ever penetrated human organs, it could cause death. Mum never felt we were safe and kept calling out to us,

"Mind the Bilharzia!"

We all evaded its dangerous penetration. Packing up the car to leave Lake Chivero was always sad. We never wanted to leave, and since it had become our only wildlife option during the war, we made the most of each visit. I have incredibly happy memories of the place, and what it meant to our family.

Stone cottages at Lake Chivero look like this - Photograph by Curtis Dahl

Male Impala with his female herd - Photography by Curtis Dahl

Avril, Les, Bill, Mum - Bill's Birthday. Hill Lodge

CHAPTER 6

Hill Lodge

The glue that holds the relationship between the leader and the led – is
trust, and trust is based on integrity
- Brian Tracy

Quality leadership is invaluable, and respect is earned. Bill and Avril Whitaker represented the gold standard in the Nobel category for mentorship.

The Whitaker family came into our lives courtesy of our mother's musical distinction. Anthony was nine, Lesley was eight, Howard was six, and Stephen and I were five. Anthony quickly qualified Les as an intelligently astute playmate, and Howard drew up new standards in physical competitiveness – so determined was he to keep up with Anthony's and Les' game planning and running speeds. He absolutely succeeded. Stephen and I ran behind them for the ride, happy just to be included.

The Whitakers' Hill Lodge home was close to ours in suburban Highlands. 'Jack, Jack, shine your light' was our favorite nighttime game, particularly in the Whitakers' never-ending garden. There were rocky terraces with slasto pathways in and out of bougainvillea bushes that transported us to hideaway places – impenetrable places with secret access codes. Anthony and Les would disappear into never-before-discovered territory that they knew we could never find. If they possessed a drill and a set of aqualungs, they would have dug a hole and swum their way down to the water table fifty feet below.

Howard's, Stephen's and my secret weapon during these 'Jack, Jack, shine your light' nights was to utilize the Whitakers' German Shepherds, Kinross and Katie. Their scent capabilities made them expert trackers. We'd extricate them from the house and set them on a mission:

"Kinross, Katie. Good dogs. Find them. Suhhhhhhh."

But Anthony and Les stopped us in our tracks - immediately reminding us that using the dogs was against the game's codes of ethics.

"You can't send the dogs after us," they'd yell from their hiding place. "That's cheating!"

Anthony or 'Amo', as we began to call him, emerged with Les from the bougainvillea bush, scratched and bleeding. They weren't about to forfeit their painful hiding efforts to our use of the dogs to ferret them out.

During the hot African days, we'd access the swimming pool at the bottom of the garden by leaping down the slasto staircase adjacent to the red-hot pokers and exotic blazes of bird of paradise plants. Once we were a few feet away from the pool, we'd have competitions to see who could perform the best acrobatic dive. Front-way dives usually scored three out of five points; backward dives scored a four or five. Howard became the comedian I had never had. Instead of scoring the highest points, he'd opt to amuse me. This athletically gifted boy would deliberately hurt himself by belly-flopping off the diving board, knowing that I would dissolve on the grass into unrestrained laughter. He'd change it up for variety. One week he'd do frog dives sideways; the next week he'd do back-hurting flops. The amusement became a staple in our friendship. Howard was the performer and I was the audience.

Just as our dad had built us a tree house, Bill built Les and Howard their own special tree house. One night, the two nature-loving children decided that the tree house was a far better place to sleep than their actual brick house, so they asked Bill and Avril if they could sleep in it. They agreed. As the night wore on, and the sounds of nocturnal animals converged closer to the tree house, Les and Howard decided that returning to the main house was probably a more sensible idea. It was their tacit acknowledgment that the wilds of Africa could not be tamed.

I had never met a sister and brother team that worked as effectively as Les and Howard's relationship did. They incentivized each other with their fiercely competitive natures, and it was always done with good humor, and supportive acknowledgment of the victor.

Christmases and New Year's Eve parties held their special cache of exquisite memories. Large sections of the Whitakers' house were cleared out to make room for food-laden buffet tables. Christmases were usually at the Addison home, while New Year's Eve was a Whitaker specialty. Avril set up the dancing music in the dining room so that we would all enjoy Scottish country dancing. Anthony's bagpipe-playing talents became a part of the celebration. By the early hours of the morning, we'd run outside, transferring our dancing energy into hiding in the garden. I remember wading into the goldfish ponds – just for fun. The green algae at the base provided a soft cushion for our bare feet, and the organic feel of fish swimming past our skin was thrilling.

On those glorious nights, both adults and children forgot about the passage of time. It was as if our passionate indulgence in life could outrun the clocks. The golden Zimbabwean sun would rise above the fir-tree line, and we'd laugh with the satisfaction that we'd defied the night's insistence that we go to bed and sleep.

Our friendship with the Whitakers went much more deeply than that. Avril became Stephen's and my speech and drama teacher. Since I had spent the first eight years of my life evaporating under Anthony's brilliant shadow, Avril seemed to possess a sixth sense in observational skills. She gently coaxed me to come out into the sun, to open my eyes widely, and to use my voice confidently with shoulders pressed firmly back. She gave me lead roles on stage when I didn't have any concept of their voluminous extent. As I fell into the responsibility of performance nights; nights that required me to rise to the occasion linguistically and pianistically, I realized that Avril's carefully curated plan of building me into something I did not know I could ever be – would serve me well later in life. Avril read me and nurtured my growth with her enormous insight and kindness.

Bill Whitaker contributed incalculable gifts to our family too. He understood my mother as I did not. We knew that she was an accomplished pianist whose world was a stage with an orchestra. She shone when she could direct the nuances of the orchestra and achieve the impossibly high standards she sought. But when that classical world was not there when she needed it, she sank into a hole that was wholly inaccessible.

Bill, a classical music connoisseur, understood how to keep mum buoyed in her rarefied auditory space. As our families socialized from November 11th, Anthony's birthday, through to January 2nd, the Whitaker's presence in our home added volumes of light-hearted good cheer.

The ozone layer changed after New Year as we anticipated mum's emotional crash. While taking down all our Christmas decorations on January 6th, the solemnity of the event mirrored the brewing black clouds and the ascent of the storm-drenched rainy season. Mum's music blocked out the noise of life, and the sounds that she couldn't tolerate. With the onset of the stormy season, it was as if the loud African thunder cracks drowned out the soothing sounds of Mozart.

There was another huge storm brewing that we chose not to notice. The Rhodesian War intensified markedly after Mozambique acquired independence from its Portuguese colonists in 1974. The liberation group, FRELIMO, was victorious, and this opened up another massive border insurgency from the east wing into our country. Our defiant Prime Minister kept appearing on our television station, claiming that the Rhodesian troops were enjoyed trouncing successes against the African liberation forces. It simply wasn't true.

"Never in my lifetime," he proclaimed, "will there be black majority rule in Rhodesia." He was 100% wrong. Even at age twelve I understood that the morality of denying 90% of our population equal opportunity and the right to vote, based on the color of their skin, was wrong.

It's at these critical junctures in our lives when the necessity for well-informed, educated adults around us becomes a turning point in our lives. By 1975, I was a hungry-for-facts teenager. Mum and dad calculated the cost of mandatory conscription of all white boys who were finishing their year of high school. As the death rates amongst Anthony's peers soared, so too did my parents' resolve to keep Anthony out of a war that was ethically flawed.

Bill, Lesley and Howard Whitaker took me to school every morning while dad had secretively gone down to South Africa to scout the prospects of moving his family down south. Bill stepped in to the breach by covering all my transportation needs to a private school far from our home.

As I climbed into the backseat of his car every morning, I was acutely aware of the double treat: the first was that we always rode in the car of my dreams, but the second, more important treat, was listening to the answers he gave me when I asked him difficult questions. I was deeply interested in the concept of African Nationalism. I wanted to understand its cause so that I could make sense of a rapidly escalating war. Bill was a High Court Judge in Rhodesia, so his information volume was vast, and his understanding of racial oppression reflected his humanity.

A few years later, in 1979, after Bill had resigned his High Court Judge position because of the untenable edicts from the minority government, Bill, Les and I drove up from South Africa to Zimbabwe in a two-day car journey. As we crossed the border into war-ravaged Zimbabwe, we realized that we had just missed the military convoy that escorted civilian vehicles on the country's main road to Harare. The army made use of anti-landmine tanks and the soldiers had their guns loaded and pointed - in case there was an attack on the road. Traveling without the convoy was too risky, so Bill pressed his foot hard on the accelerator metal – urging his car to catch up with the convoy as quickly as possible.

I stared out the window at the state of the country, and wondered how it was that our beautiful country had been reduced to this state of abject desolation. Every angle I viewed confirmed the sensory-numbing destruction.

Soldiers on both sides of the war had scorched entire African villages to the ground. It wasn't just huts that were incinerated. There were people inside those huts who were burned alive. That was the standard punishment meted out to civilians who showed allegiance to the wrong side. We could see the smoldering remnants of areas that had been charred, and I imagined the screams of the people.

Zimbabwean farms that had once fed the continent of Africa were demolished - turned into military bases. The rich, arable land lay fallow – and the people who had farmed the land were either dead, mutilated, held hostage or they fled.

As our military convoy traveled slowly in its six-hour journey across the country's main artery, it was the faces of the Zimbabwean people that scorched the deepest imprint on my memory.

A severely emaciated woman, who probably hadn't had a meal in weeks, was running feebly away from us – fearing that any association with the convoy could cause her more bloodshed. She fumbled her hands around her head – as if they'd form a protective membrane from an impending onslaught. As she stumbled in weakness, and crouched behind a bare thorn bush, I gained a small sense of her fear. She wouldn't look at us as the last flickers of her survival flame burned. Her emaciated skeleton was only two strokes away from death – and yet she still sought and held onto the last vestiges of life.

The war tattooed incalculable scars on the souls of its people – the depths of which we would never know. All Zimbabwean people had suffered immeasurable losses, and their faces were contorted from the terrifying emotional wreckage.

The Zimbabwe I had once known with children running at the sides of the roads laughing and waving at our car - was gone. Nobody waved. Nobody laughed. The conflict had anesthetized our natural human bonds. Tens of thousands of people had lost their lives in this horrific war.

I shall never forget Bill's words to me as we drove across the barren land:

"This is an absolutely tragic war, Di. The loss on both sides is immense, and it needn't have happened. There are no winners."

As the years and decades have passed, I've faced critical crossroads in my life in which I've wrestled for solutions. Not surprisingly, it's always been the words of Bill and Avril Whitaker that have come to the fore – even though I now live on the opposite end of the world. I can never thank them enough for the life rudder they provided me - the stabilizer in high seas. Bill passed away in 2005. He was a giant of a man.

As I put this book to press, Avril and Les – who now live on a farm outside Cape Town - relayed the distressing news to me that Howard had just been killed in a car accident in Abu Dhabi. The tragic irony is that he was one of the safest drivers I ever knew. As I absorbed the loss of this special man, this stalwart childhood friend, I felt that a critical component of my life had been wrenched away. Howard and I had shared a lifetime of memories, and he understood me vastly well. Losing that surety – that familiar friend who understood all my subtleties – left a significant hole in my heart.

Di with Whitakers (Howard back row 3rd from right) & Beviss-Challinors, Cape 2013

Steve, Kinross, Les, Howard, Anthony, Di, Katie - Hill Lodge Harare 1975

Avril, Howard, Les, Steve, Anthony (driving), Nancy & Phillimon. Hill Lodge 1976

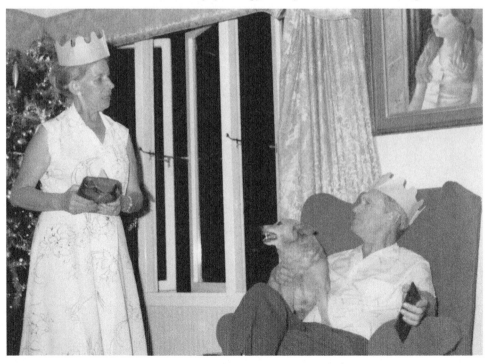

Mum, Bill, Christmas 1980

Rhodesian War - Picture courtesy selousscouts.tripod.com

Zimbabwean Villages burned to ground

Stafford Poyser, Di, Neill Hobbs (of 'A Razzle' fame) - South Africa 2016

CHAPTER 7

A Razzle

At his lips' touch she blossomed like a flower and the incarnation was complete
- F. Scott Fitzgerald: The Great Gatsby

Every culture in the world has its traditional 'coming of age' rite of passage. In the Aboriginal culture, the Australian walkabout was once considered the ultimate rite of passage. Aboriginal boys, once they reached adolescence, went off to fend for themselves in the wilderness for six months. It was considered the ultimate physical and spiritual journey.

In Africa, a bygone rite of passage amongst the Masai tribe in eastern Africa necessitated that a young man face a lion on foot in the African savanna, and kill it. To the relief of conservationists and humanitarians, that manhood-proving ritual is rarely practiced in this more modern age.

For Anthony and his classmates at the all boys Churchill High School in Harare, their sixteenth year definitively marked their 'coming of age' milestone. As their testosterone levels sky rocketed to stratospheric heights, so too did their planning prowess. "*A Razzle*" was Form 4A1's brainchild wrought from the idea of everyone in the class betting on the school's First Rugby team's performance. A syndicate was formed with Anthony navigating the Starship Enterprise. The consensus amongst the boys was that the syndicate idea had to have a sexy aura – like cigars and Dimple Haig – an upmarket version of scotch. Their marketing skills were germinating creatively.

The testosterone-charged group of sixteen-year-olds also incorporated business principles into their methodology. Just like a company with a Board of Directors, *A Razzle* had to be a legitimate event so they invited respectable adults with authority into the coming-of-age program. Their favorite teachers, Mr. Hambly and Mr. Marais, came on board.

Each boy paid in 2.4 cents; they drew up a matrix and bet on all the possible outcomes of the rugby games. By the end of the season, their remarkably accurate predictions brought in $17.50 – which in 1973 was a staggering quantity of money for schoolboys. The *A Razzle* kitty produced the revelation of early prosperity.

With success wrapped up in the bank, it was time to hold the party that they had been waiting for their entire sixteen years. Their classmate, André Stapa, held the key to the prize. He played tennis for Mashonaland (a province in Zimbabwe), and with his good looks and talent, he had access to young ladies who were not only alive - but exquisitely alive.

This was a parched group of young men who'd been isolated in XY territory way past their explosion date. It was an inconceivably exhilarating thought that a whole legion of young women with scientifically confirmed XX chromosomes was about to orbit them – come close enough for them to be even touchable – all within the following week. It was combustion Saturday; time to jumpstart their love lives at supersonic speed.

I've taught high school boys in Africa for over a decade, and that experience gives me some objectivity when describing them. I have no hesitation in knighting Churchill Boys' High School's 1973 class 4A1 as a remarkably gifted group. They may not have known it at the time, but God endowed them with extensive capabilities – not least of which was their musical knowledge and appreciation.

The poetry and social commentary of the era from artists such as Bob Dylan did not escape this intelligent group. The music for *A Razzle* was carefully curated: Carlos Santana and *Black Magic Woman*, Led Zeppelin, Deep Purple, Grand Funk, Jethro Tull's *Aqualung*, Black Sabbath, Uriah Heep, Rare Earth, and the Moody Blues were all part of a rarefied selection of rock history. Anthony was one of the best bagpipe players in Churchill school's famous Pipe Band. On his inception year, 1970, he took home the cup for the most promising player in the school. These collective musical strengths produced an evening that most credible musicians would term discerning musical choices in the history-making playbook.

Our outdoor living area in our Highlands home was the chosen stage for *A Razzle's* rocket launch. Mum's music studio had an adjoining large-covered patio that fed out onto the blue-watered swimming pool area. Our large garden around the pool was ablaze with tropical palms, colorful frangipani, pointsettia, and we had boundary-defining fir trees at the demarcation line between our property and that of our neighbor's.

I was twelve years old on the night of *A Razzle*, and I had no intention of wasting the gargantuan opportunity it presented for me to study and observe the land of burgeoning young adulthood. I was determined to get an A+ studying Act I of 4A1's coming of age, so I positioned myself strategically behind the Chinese Lantern bush – to the right of the patio. It was close enough for intricate observation, and secluded enough for me to be invisible.

Neill Hobbs was the class's natural leader. I observed the seismic effect he had on his classmates years before he went on to become Head Boy of Churchill School in 1975. Carlos Santana's *Black Magic Woman* was Neill's lion moment and Jill Leschnik was his lioness. I think that Carlos Santana would have been proud of the lion and lioness' interpretation. I know that I was both riveted and terrified as I imbibed the visual and audible expanse of the attraction between a young man and a young woman. And yet, there was more.

Act II unfolded: the lion took the lioness for a sensual stroll along the pool water's edge. It was a full-mooned night - accentuating the perfection of the garden. The lion needed trees – lots of them for camouflage and privacy - so he moved the lioness to an alcove between the fir trees. Two bodies could not have melded closer together, and my memory blacked out at that stage with no recollection of the fruition of the activities in the fir-tree lair.

This was one of the most exciting safaris I had ever witnessed, and I wanted more. I moved stealthily to the avocado tree, climbed it, and used our wooden tree house as a vantage point. The full moon provided enough light for me to observe all the intricacies. While there was a great deal of coupling going on, I recall Shirley Meiring and Sally Rivron exceling in the entertaining department. Shirley, in particular, became her own one-woman comedy show. The young Churchillians surrounded her and fell on laughter as a conduit for the conjuring emotions of the evening.

There were other friends from other schools present too; I clearly remember Dean Wood, the future Deputy Head Boy of Oriel Boys' High School bringing his levelheaded, mature presence to the party. He was always a magnet for women who wanted a piece of his solidity. Lesley Whitaker, the future Head Girl of the Dominican Convent, came in her sky blue pants, and all the characteristics that I admired about her. It was a gathering quite unlike anything I would ever see again.

As the close-to-midnight hour approached, Anthony took it up a notch by playing the Moody Blues' *Nights in White Satin* - switching off all the lights at the request of his friends, who were making significant headway with their XX chromosomal partners. I knew that doing this would never fly with mum. Within minutes she stormed onto the patio and ordered Anthony to turn on the lights. It was yet another crackling showdown between two headstrong people. Mum was determined to limit the romantic possibilities that transgressed her ethical boundaries, and Anthony was going to pursue his goals without any capitulation.

And yet the clash between mum and Anthony was not what I remembered most about that night. Just as African lions have always mesmerized me – held my attention with their irrepressible spirits – the inextinguishable dreams of 1973's 4A1 class gave me the rapturous assurance that life's infinite possibilities could be pursued at full throttle. I'd been given this rare opportunity to vicariously feed off the boys' zeal, and it filled me with enough hope to ignite my own engine. With conviction and passion, this group could go to Mars and back without trepidation.

Tragically, some of them lost their lives while soaring. André Stapa, the well-loved, handsome classmate who had invited most of the young women to *A Razzle*, barely made it much past this coming-of-age milestone. After being conscripted into the Rhodesian Air Force during the country's fifteen-year war that finally ended in 1980, his skills were enlisted in South Africa to fight the insurgency against the South West African People's Organization (SWAPO). While flying for the South African Air Force over the area which is known as Namibia today, the Impala jet he was piloting was shot down. After somebody witnessed the massive explosion, the control tower lost all contact with André. He perished – leaving behind a young son, Tarquin.

*A Razzle's party grounds - Addison Home Zimbabwe - now derelict -
Di's visit back in 2013*

'A Razzle' played plenty of Led Zeppelin

Mum, Clara, Rani, Skippy – Cadogan Drive

CHAPTER 8

War and Emigration

War is what happens when language fails
- **Margaret Atwood**

Unlike Leo Tolstoy's famous novel, *War and Peace*, the Addison family's journey was War and Emigration. With the obituary list of young eighteen-year-old boys losing their lives to the Rhodesian War filling up our local newspaper columns in increasingly alarming numbers, dad was intent upon extricating Anthony from a future obituary list. Every time our black phone rang, I winced with dread at the familiar sound that corroborated the frightening statistics of the war's casualties.

We did not go gently into that good night. After Form 4A1's *A Razzle* party, and Anthony's lights-off defiance, mum responded with intransigence. With no psychological tools to navigate an intelligent sixteen-year-old into calmer waters, she bore down on Anthony with iron force.

"This is *my* roof, and as long as you are living under it, you'll obey *my* rules."

When Anthony smirked at the rules and locked himself in his bedroom, mum ramped up the disciplinary measures with threats of boarding school.

"Falcon College is where you'll go for your last two years of school. They'll teach you how to respect your mother."

Falcon College was three hundred miles away. Since we were gearing up towards the peak of a devastating war, I'm not sure how mum planned to drive Anthony there. There were military skirmishes and landmines everywhere. Was she planning to drive around the war?

Most of the confidence-building progress I had made with Avril Whitaker dissipated that year. As I cowered at home, I confronted a new enemy: intense, blinding migraines. I'd sit in class at the Dominican Convent, and as the teacher's shape in front of me became fuzzy, like the black and white dots on a funky television screen, I realized that one of those three-day migraines was on its way. They blinded me mercilessly, and friends had to lead me to the school sickbay because I couldn't see.

On my non-migraine days, the social dynamics of my school, the Dominican Convent, represented the first reckoning I had of our tragic war. Sitting in the desk next to me was Gladys Chavunduka, the daughter of Dr. Gordon Chavunduka, a powerful Zimbabwean politician and academic who, at the time, was a critical leader in the country's war and its fight for justice. You didn't need to be a rocket scientist to understand that he was leading the black liberation forces.

Also in our class was Elizabeth Smith, the country's Deputy Prime Minister's daughter. I'd watch from the trees next to our school's huge golden gates as Elizabeth arrived in her very important dad's official black Mercedes-Benz – driven by a chauffeur wearing a smart black cap. Perched proudly on the radio antenna was the country's green and white flag. The policemen at our school gates jumped to military attention and saluted the car, even though Deputy Prime Minister David was often absent. I guess they were ordered to salute the car because it was a very important vehicle – with or without the actual Deputy Prime Minister.

Elizabeth sat at the other end of our classroom – away from Gladys. There was an aura of absurdity about the whole sorry situation. Their fathers were in a bloody war against each other, and yet they were sitting in the same school classroom. I wondered if that was the reason that Gladys' father never accompanied her to school, because the policemen might want to shoot him as his car arrived at our school's golden gates. Smart thinking.

As I pondered the complexities of the political and social situation, I decided to pretend that I was a United Nations peacekeeping officer. As Gladys and Elizabeth worked around a bitter dividing line, and just as an argument about the social injustices of the country spilled over in class, I stood up dramatically in a clumsy attempt to placate the dissention:

"I have a white flag. Let there be peace!"

If only it were that easy. Dad disappeared down to South Africa for a three-month reconnaissance trip while mum held the fort back home - barely so. Much to my relief, the Falcon College banishment for Anthony was dropped, and I was glad to have my big brother man the house during dad's absence.

Anthony, Stephen and I were instructed by mum to appear purposefully vague if anybody asked questions about our father's absence.

"Where's your dad? How come he's been gone so long?"

"He's vacationing in South Africa," we'd reply. "He's had a stressful time at work, and he needs to unwind properly for a few months." Nobody bought it.

You'd think that we were being mentally prepared for the massive changes that were about to hit our lives. Not so. They hit us like a tsunami force. It began with mum's rapidly declining physical and mental health while dad was away.

Our much-loved Dalmatian dog, Clara, had gone missing, despite our escape-tight gates and fences. As search parties went out to find her, calling 'C-L-A-R-A' all over the neighborhood, mum disintegrated. We knew that she had been recently diagnosed with advanced emphysema from cigarette smoking, but we deduced that a sprightly woman in her forties must surely be able to rise above the breathlessness. The malady was for old people only.

As Clara's disappearance marched into its third day, mum became hysterically distressed. We tried to do our part by combing Highlands on our bicycles. We rode around earnestly, calling our favorite dog's name. Surely she'd respond to us. But she didn't.

Returning after a fruitless search, we went into our parents' room to check up on mum. She was lying on her bed – her Mediterranean-olive-skin now a ghostly white – and she wasn't breathing. Anthony took charge while I ran to the glass sliding doors facing the swimming pool. I thumped my fists hard on the glass and yelled, "Please can someone help us. Our mother is dead!"

I have no recollection of the arrival of doctors or ambulances after that. My central nervous system shut down. I think that Anthony handed me over to whomever the adult was that arrived. Mum survived, and the story meted out to me a few weeks later was that she had suffered a severe asthma attack, and that was why she had stopped breathing. I didn't buy it.

Emigration D-day arrived. Every component of this encroaching reality conflicted with our hearts' desires. How do you tell a child whose life is idyllic that their lifestyle has to end because of a war? When refugees leave a war zone it's usually because life has become dangerously unbearable. Life within the confines of Highlands was tolerable - despite the impositions of Martial Law. It took an adult's vantage point to see the big picture: that the war was fast ratcheting into one of the world's worst civil wars.

With our dogs – including Clara whom we later found - and cats safely with us in the convoy of cars, I kept thinking about the movie, *The Incredible*

Journey. The tortoises didn't join us because somebody ventured onto our property and turned them into tortoise soup. We found the evidence of their empty shells lying at the bottom of the garden, near the compost heap. I shook my head in indignation at the ignoble death they suffered.

We bade farewell to an exceptionally special country and crossed the border from Zimbabwe into South Africa. Lesley Whitaker gave me a beautiful silver bracelet with valuable words engraved on it. It was my first reckoning of our bond. I waved goodbye to my little sister, Laura Landau, as if I'd see her the following day at our piece of paradise, the Umwinsidale waterfall. To this day, I have recurring dreams about the Umwinsidale waterfall – always with a rope around my waist - pulling me back from being able to reach it. When people and places infiltrate your soul profoundly, they find a soft nesting place in your heart.

My past history with hot, sticky places exacerbated the challenging circumstances ahead of us. Raw memories of monkeys biting us in Beira and the pirate-infested Indian Ocean came tumbling back. We arrived in Durban, South Africa at the peak of summer when most Durbanites themselves will advise you that the humidity is exceedingly uncomfortable. I so desperately wanted to lift the heavy gray glue air and pierce it with a device that would create open access to the blue sky above. When I tried to comfort our Siamese cats in my room that night, their desperate howling confirmed to me that they were as distressed as I was.

Mum's unhappiness intensified. Her Bluthner grand piano was in storage at the top of our garage because our new house wasn't large enough to accommodate it. Refugees from war-torn regions of the world don't transfer their assets to equal standards of living elsewhere. They take a massive economical hit. My parents' bank accounts were frozen in Zimbabwe – an emergency measure imposed by the government to prevent the massive exodus of currency out of the country. It's not right but that's what desperate countries do during times of war. Every night we'd listen to mum's sad refrain:

"My magnificent Bluthner piano is lying on its side in a storage box. What has life come to?"

It wasn't a laughing matter because we understood her priorities. Nobody in Durban knew her. If she wanted to pursue teaching in South Africa, she'd have to start from scratch and build up her reputation. I committed the unforgivable mistake of suggesting to her that she could work for a ballet company, and play the piano for the ballerinas. She threw a missile at me. All I remember is ducking.

Anthony, to his credit, made a concerted effort to help my parents. He spent hours building professional-looking wooden shelves in the closet underneath the stairwell. He proudly announced to mum that she could store all her groceries in this converted pantry space. But his generosity also came with a request: he wanted his own bedroom. There was a spare room downstairs with a bathroom and he wanted to move in there. Mum wouldn't even entertain the idea. The "no" blow hit him with zero room for negotiation.

That definitive obstructiveness in mum was a sign that she was cracking open. I studied the piano under her in Goldilocks and the Three Bears land. Despite never having the advantage of regular piano lessons like other students enjoyed, I was expected to bring home the gold plate at examination time. As we drove to our local post office to retrieve the examination results from London, mum would proudly announce,

"Well done, Diana. Top marks again. Let's go and buy you a new pair of shoes."

I knew that a full-force explosion was imminent in Durban when I sat down for a piano lesson on a stiflingly sticky day that reminded me of that dreadfully humid afternoon in *The Great Gatsby*, where Myrtle Wilson cracks mentally, runs into the road, and is killed by Daisy Buchanan. Mum was about to teach me a new Bach piece but she was irascible and I was frustrated.

"No, Diana. Do it *this* way. Wrong, wrong, wrong."

She snapped – not minimally - but volcanically. My purple music book was torn into angry shreds and tossed out the window.

Two weeks later, dad was enjoying the fellowship of the South African reserve navy.

Anthony, Stephen and I sat down to dinner, and mum served us fried eggs. One of us complained about having breakfast at night, and mum responded by hurtling a few plates against the wall. She stormed upstairs and slammed her bedroom door shut.

An hour later, Anthony signaled to me that we should check in on mum. She'd locked the door, and that spelled trouble. Anthony prized the door open using some magical tool, and we found mum slumped on the floor, unconscious, with barely any pulse.

We carried her dead-weighted body down the stairs while somebody screamed. After loading her into the red Ranger, Anthony instructed me to sit in the back seat of the car so I could hold mum's tongue. My swift-thinking older brother drove at wind speed to Durban's Addington Hospital with a magnificent sense of responsibility. If the police stopped us for speeding, we had reasonable evidence to mitigate the fine. Once mum was transferred to the hospital gurney, we released her to an oxygen mask and the stomach-pumping equipment that saved her life.

Stephen and I were only thirteen years old and Anthony was seventeen. The events of that night went painfully deep. We left the hospital without our mother, and we did not know if we'd still have one in the morning.

Around midnight that night, the hospital called our home to give us the relieving news that mum's stomach had been fully pumped, and that she was recuperating under sedation. There was no follow-up psychiatric treatment available. Mum was simply sent home, and we were expected to absorb the after-shock with no professional guidance.

We spent eleven months in a house in which we became the worst versions of ourselves. It was on one of Durban's noisiest streets, but that was the least of our troubles. Mum was a walking time bomb, and as we tiptoed around her in fearful trepidation, we turned inwards and created our own individual air-raid shelters. The crisis forced three sensitive children to confront what people do when they feel trapped – unable to escape the sense of harrowing desperation that becomes their crippling prison.

That exceptionally dark period appeared to have a finite date, and that's the restorative beauty of life. The nights eventually end, and the sun rises in the morning with promises of better tomorrows. We sold the house that held haunting memories for our family, and moved to a home that we all loved – Cadogan Drive. Its large garden gave us a small slice of the life we had known in Goldilocks and the Three Bears land.

Even more promisingly, we discovered that Russell Argue, one of Anthony's Churchillian school friends from Harare, had also moved to South Africa – into Anthony's class at Northlands Boys' School. We were not alone. There were familiar friendships, a sense of solidarity in numbers, and a shared confrontation of the challenges ahead. At Northlands Girls' School, Karen Wilson became my close friend and confidante. She, too, was from Zimbabwe, and I couldn't have asked for a friend with greater integrity. I counted every blessing that came my way.

Di - University of Natal

CHAPTER 9

University and New Horizons

What sculpture is to a block of marble, education is to the human soul
- Joseph Addison

I was seventeen years old when I was accepted into Natal University (now known as the University of Kwa-Zulu Natal), South Africa, and that is where I transformed into a dolphin. I covered hundreds of laps in the university's huge swimming pool every week, and felt like an unstoppable baby dolphin with a strong thorax and flippers that propelled me with newly honed strength. I squeaked, blew bubbles and flourished.

With my university education financially covered by a strong set of 12th grade academic results, I dove into the university's campus lifestyle by moving into John Bews residence for girls. Anthony attended the same university as a day student, and we'd see each other on campus almost daily. At night he went home to Cadogan Drive while I stayed on campus until the weekends.

The Rhodesian/Zimbabwean War had just ended with the Lancaster House Agreement, and the young survivors from that war cascaded into the men's residences. They wore tight-green Jimmy Connors mini shorts that accentuated their strong gluteal muscles, and their feet were wrapped in brown bush shoes known as 'veldskoens.' Many of them kept their unshaven war look, and I discovered something new: I was attracted to the hairy look.

The Zimbabwean students gravitated to each other like a pod of dolphins. Since psychology was one of my university subjects, I wanted to study the mysteries of this group – long before post-traumatic stress disorder was a better-studied phenomenon. I'd visit my male friends in their residence rooms, and the not-so-subtle references to war would smack me in the stomach.

"Why do you have that cap pinned to your notice board?" I'd ask. "Is that your cap? Why does it have remnants of dried blood on it?"

"You can't ask me that question," was the secretive reply. "Stuff happened."

In John Bews residence, within one hour of moving into my room, I met Norma Walls from Canada. Her huge smile won my attention immediately, and she sat down on my bed cross-legged as if she'd known me for years.

I was so invigorated by my newly formed friendships that I turned my residence room into a beach haven – a relaxed place where we could all gather after the day's lectures and share our human warmth together. I brought in a bamboo-boxed real palm tree, and emulated beach sand by plopping down a soft white carpet. Even a gold fish named 'Harry' joined us. A welcoming tray with fresh pineapple juice was on tap for anybody who wished to visit my room, and add greater layers of happiness to my already well-satisfied quotient.

And come they did. Dad kindly lent me a small television for my room, and since I was the only girl in residence with my own television set, girls lined up to watch *Dallas* and *Dynasty* in my room. I had a small chalkboard pinned to my door, and the first people who wrote their names on the board won the coveted Tuesday or Thursday night treat. Nine was the limit I could squash into my beach room.

Dad's generosity also included a set of Jensen speakers for the music that he knew I loved so well. I broke away from Beethoven and Schubert, and dared to indulge in Queen, Steve Perry and Journey, The Alan Parsons Project, and Tom Petty and the Heartbreakers. *Refugee* became one of our anthems during our 5 – 6 pm noise hour. My rock music collection turned our residence corridor into a veritable *Rock & Roll Hall of Fame* emporium.

When Norma Walls and Michelle King gathered into my room at night, I'd mellow down the tempo to Phil Collins' *In the Air Tonight* or Jim Croce's *Time in a Bottle*. The words seemed to fit so appropriately with this intoxicatingly special time in our lives. When I'd play Barbara Streisand's *Woman in Love*, Norma and Michelle would sing along - changing the words to, "Diana is a Woman in Love", although I definitely wasn't in love with any man at that stage. All three of us lay on our backs, fitting so perfectly together on my pink and white comforter. I couldn't imagine any other comforter in the world accommodating as much joy as this one absorbed.

As summer peeped around the corner, our Zimbabwean group did an annual boat ride aboard the *Jolly Roger*. This sparsely equipped boat was cheap to rent, and we could pretend that we were on some exotic cruise ship as we glided around Durban harbor. Norma and I were glued to each other's energy, and we protected each other's backs loyally. And yet, there was a chink in the happiness armor even then.

During one of our group's rides from the *Jolly Roger* back to university residence, one of the young men fell from the back of the Land Rover in which he was traveling. He was killed instantly. The irony is that he survived a brutal war in Zimbabwe, but was killed in the safety of South Africa, riding home from a boat party.

When the Christmas holidays descended upon us, Norma invited me to her parents' dairy farm in the tiny African country of Swaziland. The Swazi government had enlisted the help of her Canadian father to assist them with the latest farming techniques.

As Norma and I boarded the train for the overnight journey to Swaziland, I felt like Meryl Streep riding in a similar train in the movie *Out of Africa* where she calls out to Robert Redford, "how far are you traveling?" My journey-filled life was charting up another exciting chapter. As we choo-chooed our way across the lush Ezulwini Valley into Swaziland, I felt a combustible sense of elation. Norma's Canadian family met us at the train station, and I rejoiced at the opportunity of meeting new parents and friends from diverse backgrounds.

Norma's parents didn't stay long. They were called back to Canada to attend some conference, so Norma and I were charged with staying on the Swazi farm, and attending to any farmworkers' problems. We were eighteen years old. Piece of cake, we thought.

That night, Norma and I were invited to a farm party twenty miles away. We took her parents' bright blue Datsun out at around 9pm. En route to the party, Norma complained that the car's accelerator wasn't responding to her foot presses. I looked concerned as the car chugged to a spluttering crawl. Within two minutes, the engine stalled. Norma was convinced that there was a mechanical problem with the accelerator; it didn't appear to be an empty gas reason. There we were – two young girls in darkest Africa - in the middle of nowhere with a car that had failed us. There were no cell phones, nobody in sight, and no cars driving past. When Africa is quiet, it's deafeningly quiet.

We huddled in the car while making a resolute decision that it was wise to sleep in the car – and wait for the surety of the morning sun. I'd sleep in the back seat area, and Norma would take up the front. As we congratulated ourselves on our sensibility, the plan went awry.

An army truck approached with a load of drunk-sounding soldiers aboard. They slowed down, and the sound of their engine felt like a dangerous convergence. These were not military personnel protecting the public. This was a ramshackle group of rowdy soldiers in camouflage gear, shouting and behaving extraordinarily badly. Norma and I whispered to each other,

"Don't let them see us. Grab a blanket, a jacket, whatever. Cover yourself!"

Whenever I watch the movie *Blood Diamond*, particularly the scene where Leonardo DiCaprio tries to hide in the jungle when he hears the sound of a noisy, soldier-filled truck approaching, I am transported right back to Swaziland that night. It was menacing. Experience accrues wisdom, and it shouted at me in that vulnerable moment.

Without flashlights, the men couldn't really see if there was anything interesting in our car, so they began to accelerate away from us. I could feel my heart beating like a base drum in my chest.

"We can't stay here," I said, "they'll come back later. I see a light at the top of that hill. There must be a farm in that direction. Follow me."

We slid out of the car like two frightened animals. The night was darker than I had ever known, and the wild African grass was taller than was safe. Anything could hide in it without our knowing. With courage or stupidity firmly intact, Norma and I climbed through two lines of barbed wire fencing, and began our sprint through the long grass – carefully assessing how to land our feet so that our ankles didn't buckle if there was a hole in the ground. With adrenalin driving us, we willed ourselves towards the light.

"It's just a short distance from here. We're almost there."

Right at the utterance of those words, a pair of furious-faced Doberman dogs came bounding down the hill towards us. Many farmers in southern Africa keep Dobermans as fierce guardians of their properties. Dogs smell fear and it makes them more aggressive. I ran ahead of Norma and called out to the dogs as if they were my own. Frankly, I was relieved to see them.

"Hello my boys," I called out in a soothing voice. "Good dogs. Come to mummy. Aren't you such good boys?" My tone changed when I said firmly, "Now sit!"

As the Doberman brothers screeched to a halt, I saw the foamy saliva in their mouths turn to wet glob sliding down their jaws. My responsive instincts had worked.

Our good fortune extended. The farmhouse was inhabited by an elderly farmer who came out from his house, appeared confused at first, and then called his dogs to his heels. We were safe. The caring man gave us a place to sleep, and a ride back to our farm the following morning.

My visit to Swaziland had a lot more action in store. A week later, as I bade farewell to Norma at Mbabane airport, I became so swept up by the general bon vivant atmosphere in the airport that my logical faculties vacated their post.

"Bye, bye, Norma," I called out as I swooped to the next action station.

I'd already become acquainted with a young Australian wearing a straw hat, and as he started to walk across the airport's tarmac, I followed him with considerable friendliness. We boarded a Royal Swazi Fokker F28 jet on the runway, and I did the perfunctory ticket show to the flight attendant at the top of the stairs. She smiled at me broadly and I felt very adult-like – very in control of my activity-charged life.

After fastening our seatbelts, the Fokker F28 jet took off at a considerably steep gradient after traversing a very short runway. I figured that maybe they had run out of the materials to finish the runway properly. Thirty minutes into the flight, the captain announced on the speakers that the staff would be serving lunch. That's odd, I thought. The flight was only supposed to be one hour to Durban. How were they going to serve lunch after thirty minutes, have us eat, and pack up before we landed? I thought I'd better check on the details. When the flight attendant, Pinky, walked past me in her smart white and navy uniform, I said,

"This flight is en route to Durban, correct?" Pinky responded with a nod and a smile that would have made any dentist proud.

Two hours into the flight, I realized with absolute certainty that we weren't on our way to Durban. I turned to the tourist behind me and asked courteously, "Sir, are we flying to Durban?"

"No, London, actually. But we will still stop off in Kenya. And I believe we're making a pit stop in Malawi before then."

I moved like a lightning bolt out of my seat and towards the cockpit – which was unlocked in the days before 9/11.

"Pinky, I need to speak with the pilot, please."

Captain Farquharson emerged from the airplane's flying headquarters and read the problem in my face immediately. To his considerable credit, he didn't respond emotionally.

"Oh dear," he said. "Here's the plan. We will land in Blantyre, Malawi in a few hours. I can drop you off there, and we'll pick you up in three days' time. Find a hotel and make yourself comfortable."

I didn't have any money on me. The little I did have I had spent in Swaziland, and dad was supposed to be picking me up at Durban airport, so why would I have any money on me? Furthermore, my luggage was not on board the Fokker F28. It was tagged for Durban on the right flight. It carried my change of clothes, and since the jeans I was wearing would ban me from landing in Muslim Malawi, the plan was derailed on multiple fronts.

"That means you will be staying with us," said Captain Farquharson decisively. "We will be flying into Kenya tonight, and staying at the InterContinental Hotel in Nairobi. We will take care of you there, and when we eventually fly back to Swaziland, you will return with us."

Everything about this kind captain's demeanor turned a precarious situation into one of my best lifetime memories. Captain Farquharson invited me to join he and his co-pilot in the airplane's cockpit. There was a jump seat between them, and he promised to let me see how they flew the plane.

My gratitude for the invite ricocheted into the exosphere when I laid eyes on the Fokker F28's co-pilot. Never before had my eyes drunk in a member of the XY chromosomal species with such appreciation. Mr. Co-Pilot was scintillatingly gorgeous, rapturously pleasing to all my senses. My skin tickled, my heart swelled, my cheeks burned with heated anticipation. Even the three stripes on Mr. Co-Pilot's broad-shouldered lapels were the best three stripes and lapels I had ever seen! They gleamed with masculinity and prominence; shone with importance. How could my day's stupidity have turned into something so fantastic?

As Mr. Co-Pilot helped Captain Farquharson land the jet in equatorially drenched Malawi, I marveled at his super-human qualities – landing the plane in thunderous conditions. Even the flock of birds that appeared to hit one of our wings didn't deter Mr. Co-Pilot from achieving the impossible. He soared through all the difficulties. I was so swept up by his brilliance that I wanted him to fly me to the moon. We didn't need Captain Farquharson to come with us. I wanted to fly, fly, fly away with this supreme manhood hunk.

By nightfall we reached Kenya where a distinct problem presented itself. I was on a South African passport, and because of apartheid, I wasn't allowed to enter Kenya. Captain Farquharson ordered me to put on the spare flight attendant's uniform. If it meant that I could spend more time with Mr. Co-Pilot, I was willing to wear anything. Captain Farquharson told the passport control authorities that I was a trainee crewmember, and that I didn't always carry a passport with me. He said he'd remind to do so next trip.

It was as easy as that. I swept into Kenya with accomplishment written all over my hormone-charged face. As we boarded the taxi with the scary driver who only used two wheels to speed around corners, I feared not – for Mr. Co-Pilot could provide wings - whatever we needed to prevent the taxi from toppling over.

The brass lettering of the InterContinental Hotel gleamed especially brightly that night. I swooshed my dolphin carriage up the hotel stairs and waited importantly at the marble reception desk. I was proud to announce that I was a member of Mr. Co-Pilot's crew.

That night, after a star-struck dinner in which I only managed to fork four carrots on my plate, Captain Farquharson invited me to join Mr. Co-Pilot, Pinky and himself at a dance club. In an attempt to modify my obvious ecstasy, I rolled my tongue around my mouth to enhance the casual response:

"That sounds like a plan. I guess that would work."

In preparation for our euphoric night out on Nairobi's throbbing streets, Mr. Co-Pilot dropped all formalities by changing out of his Royal Swazi uniform into Levi jeans and a crisp white shirt. My temperature soared to fever level. I determined that if I died that night – I would have left the earth on life's ultimate climax.

As I strode past the marble reception desk of the InterContinental Hotel in a pair of jeans that were about to experience the best night of their well-worn life - I gave a dramatic wave to the concierge desk in case they never saw me again.

"Good night, everyone! Thank you for EVERYTHING, " I called out.

My patient father, who had waited at Durban airport anticipating my arrival, was eventually informed only after we landed in Kenya, that I had caught the wrong airplane. Later that night, he tried calling me in my hotel room, but I was shaking my derrière in a Nairobi nightclub with Mr. Co-Pilot.

I apologized to Royal Swazi Air a few days later, only after Mr. Co-Pilot, Captain Farquharson and I spent a blissful day together in the cockpit – flying back to Swaziland. All three of us wore green aviator sunglasses, and I could not have felt more proud of the expedition's success.

Dad received the biggest apology. He explained to me later how the airport delivered the news to him:

"Your daughter boarded the plane in Mbabane, Mr. Addison, but it appears that she has not landed with the plane here in Durban."

Dad replied, "Did she parachute out of the window?"

I will, however, remain eternally grateful to Mr. Co-Pilot for awakening XX hormones I never knew I had.

My closest friends have asked me if Mr. Co-Pilot and I kept in contact afterwards. I'm sorry to be the bearer of disappointing news but the answer is - no. He was far more testosterone than I knew how to handle so I ran back to my chaste world and its accompanying pink and white comforter. I had changed, though, and only later would I discover the fruits of that transformation.

Di and Chris. Jolly Roger Boat 1982

Steve and Di cutting 21st birthday cake

Steve and Di - 21st speech

Michelle King (center)

Guy Palmer, Natal University

Mum and Di

Cadogan Drive Waterfall

Stafford Poyser (left)

CHAPTER 10

Transkei and Cadogan Confluence

We must strive to be moved by a generosity of spirit that will enable us to outgrow the hatred and conflicts of the past.
- Nelson Mandela

Nelson Mandela, the greatest statesman of the 20th century, was born in the remote district of Transkei in the southeastern part of South Africa. The Xhosa people – Mandela's tribe - occupied the territory, and from 1976 to 1994, during apartheid's slow but inevitable demise, it was an unrecognized state. This information is an important backdrop to Dr. Bob Poyser because of the role he played during the dark apartheid era.

Hugh Stafford Poyser, known affectionately as Bob, spent extensive years training to be a medical doctor, and along the way, he met his life partner, Denise Poyser. This tight marital unit settled in the Transkei region, and Dr. Bob Poyser immediately became the saving grace of the beleaguered Transkei people. Apartheid cut them off from the rest of the South African economy, and their daily struggles were mountainous.

Hundreds of desperately poor people lined up outside Dr. Poyser's surgery every day, and even though most of them had no money to pay for his services, he healed them anyway. Even the local traditional witch doctor turned to Dr. Poyser with these words: "I treat the mind. You treat the body. Please help me."

The local villagers showed their immense gratitude by building their doctor an airplane runway so that he could fly sick patients to big city hospitals in times of emergency. When Dr. Poyser died in 1987, thousands of African people showed their respects by lining the streets of Transkei. Their grief was as palpably raw as the Poyser family's grief.

Bob and Denise's son, Stafford George Poyser, was, and still is, an exceptionally gifted athlete who became one of South Africa's top rugby players. (Rugby in South Africa is the American hierarchal equivalent of football.) After helping his school rugby team dominate the leadership boards across the country, Stafford graduated from St. Andrew's College in South Africa, and began his next academic chapter at Natal University (University of Kwa-Zulu Natal).

I met Stafford Poyser at our university's swimming pool when I was eighteen years old. I had just completed my late afternoon swimming session, and as my monkey arms lifted my body out of the water, and I dripped my way to the waiting towel, Stafford's and my eyes locked – just like in the movies. KA-BAMMMMM! His golden tan showcased a set of rippling muscles. His skin glistened like that of the Greek gods. I felt immediately grateful to Mr. Co-Pilot of Fokker F28 jet in Swaziland. Only a month earlier, he had jump-started my XX hormones. I had absolutely no idea what to do with the hormonal elicitation, but feeling the magnetic attraction to the XY species was a promising starting point.

I blame myself entirely for the amusing but clumsy foreplay that followed. All I knew was how to be a dolphin, so Stafford and I swam, and we swam, and we swam! We did cartwheels into the pool, and swam at its base like lobsters foraging the ocean's crust. When the sun's angle created that magical pre sunset hour, we lay around the pool, strategically placing our bodies at angles that we knew were complimentary to our stomachs, thighs and buttocks. It was all about body-part accentuation back then.

I tried to look like the blonde bombshell from the movie *Caddyshack* by lipping my lips enticingly – as if Stafford were Chevy Chase. I don't think it worked, although Stafford did re-position himself by lying on his right side, giving me his six-pack abdominal muscle view. His stomach was so hard that I could have used it as my diving board.

When I watched Stafford play rugby for our university, he sped like Usain Bolt down the field. No wonder he had that mighty six-pack stomach. Frustratingly, or fortuitously for both of us, the foreplay remained just that initially as we played delicately around the attraction. All of that changed later as the natural forces of full-throttle physical attraction superseded our restraint.

Cadogan Drive was our family's home in Durban. Mum and dad had built the pool of our dreams by creating a rockery and waterfall around it. Anthony, Stephen and I were so grateful. On the weekends, when I joined the family at home, we'd spend the majority of our time poolside where our barbecue lifestyle was extraordinary. Mum's homemade barbecue sauce was legendary, and I slapped it on everything: fish, eggs, spinach, potatoes. Everything tasted better with mum's barbecue sauce.

At night, I'd station myself on the rock where the lip of the waterfall lay. It became my subliminal re-creation of the Umwinsidale Waterfall in Goldilocks and the Three Bears land. I had the best of both worlds: the dynamic young company I sought at my university residence during the weekdays, and our Cadogan Drive weekend oasis for quieter, calmer times. Even my aversion to the heat and humidity changed. I stayed underwater as often as I could, and always walked around with long wet hair. Durban's weather had become tolerable as I learned to assimilate it into my DNA.

Mum and dad enjoyed one of the best phases of their marriage during our Cadogan Drive years, and it gave me my first sense of peace since our immigration to South Africa. Both mum and dad were so hospitable - welcoming friends to their home from all corners of the world. As more refugees with unfathomable losses came tumbling down to South Africa from Zimbabwe, mum and dad gave them food and comfort. Elaine and Michael Morgan had lost their eldest son, Christopher, to the war. In mum and dad they found kindred souls, and a Sunday evening place of refuge. I'd watch Elaine's gentle eyes as she conversed animatedly with mum, and then I'd watch her thumb stroke her son Christopher's cigarette lighter, and read the inextinguishable pain in her heart.

Life produces extraordinary convergences. The Tudor-designed house next door to our home acquired new owners. Within months, they built a squash court on the property – right next to mum's music studio. My parents expressed their objection to the court's proximity to our boundary line. Mum felt it would interfere with the quality of her students' music lessons. "Squash balls bouncing ten feet away are not conducive to musical sound quality," she emphasized. That was the last word I heard on the topic.

One Sunday, while I was floating in our blissfully cool pool, I heard a familiar voice. That's strange, I thought. That's a voice from university. I went over to the boundary hedge to spy through it: Stafford was standing right there in all his Greek-god-like glory.

"Staf," I yelled. "What are you doing next door to us? Do you know the people who own the house?"

"My parents are the owners," he replied matter-of-factly.

Dr. and Mrs. Poyser had bought the Tudor house next door to us, and I had no knowledge of the latest development during the squash court debates.

What followed was my supreme coming-of-age. When Staf and I were home from our various activities across the country, we couldn't wait to squeeze every opportunity out of our neighborly good fortune. Our housekeeper, Elizabeth, made it really easy for us. Fittingly, she fell in love with the Poysers' gardener, and they built a wooden stile over our tall hedge so that they could access each other effortlessly without having to walk around the two properties.

Staf and I spent our university and school summer vacations poolside. It was irrelevant whose pool we lay next to, as long as we were together. Our young hearts propelled our inexhaustible energy. Long days in the sun osmotically slid into balmy tropical evenings that fed our extraordinary passion. While watching the stars and the planets in the sky, we'd revel in the rapturous unity of our optimism. Staying up all night became a vital reflection of our desire to extract every sensorial moment out of life.

As the sun rose in the morning, Staf would cross over the hedge, and go home to sleep. I'd ascend the stairs to my own sanctuary, close the window drapes, and slip into contented dreamland. It was so satisfyingly perfect – a period in our lives where pleasure flooded our banks generously.

When Nelson Mandela was released from prison after spending twenty-seven years of his life behind bars, he led all South Africans towards the termination of the oppressive apartheid years. In 1994 he became the President of a free nation.

Stafford went on to graduate from law school and became a highly successful attorney. He was part of the Transkei Attorneys Association when Cape Town attempted to take their deeds office away from them. As a result, he headed up the committee that approached Nelson Mandela for help. When Stafford met Mandela, he said with genuine respect,

"It's an honor to meet you, Mr. President."

Nelson Mandela responded with this humility: "No, it's an honor to meet you, Mr. Poyser."

Stafford's dad would have been enormously proud of his son.

In 2016, I flew out to South Africa, to the picturesque wine country of French Huguenot-pioneered Franschhoek. Serendipitously, Staf flew out from Sydney for a law conference in nearby Stellenbosch.

Staf visited me in Franshhoek, and as I watched the sixteen-seat white taxi approach my mountain cottage – throwing up plumes of red dust in its climb - my girlhood giggle returned. We hadn't seen each other in almost thirty years, but it felt like time had suspended its march.

As he emerged from the front seat of the dust-laden taxi, I saw the twenty-year-old Staf - the man who had provided me enough sense of safety in my student days - to understand that it was safe to cross the Rubicon into womanhood. The gift he gave me was priceless.

Cadogan Drive House

Bill, Basil, Doreen, Mum, Avril - Poolside Cadogan Drive

Mum's hospitalty at Cadogan Drive. Tony and Humphrey Quenet and Di.

Howard, Di, Les, Steve – Cadogan Drive poolside

Nelson Mandela

Stafford visits Di in Franschhoek, South Africa, 2016

Mum playing her Bluthner grand piano - Cadogan Drive

CHAPTER 11

Music and Mum

And Still I Rise
- Maya Angelou

Mum was a musical genius. Her acceptance into London's Royal Academy of Music was their tacit acknowledgment of her talent and work ethic. Her subsequent musical achievements were gargantuan.

Our home was filled with the sounds of Beethoven, Chopin, Schubert, Bach and Mozart. On Saturday afternoons, mum held musical appreciation classes and through them, I came to understand the magnificence behind Bach's Brandenburg Concertos. Every time I hear Brandenburg Concerto No. 4 in G, I see mum taking out her conductor's baton in solidarity with Bach's expectations of his masterpiece.

Mum's favorite performance piece was Frédéric Chopin's Etude in A-flat major, Opus 25. She caressed the arpeggios on the ebony and ivory keys with the requisite strength and artistic sensitivity that Chopin required. She never banged the piano; she coaxed it into producing definitive sounds with the nuances of her delicate touch. As she did this, I'd turn my head sideways so that my ear had closer proximity to the heavenly sound.

When mum attracted the best sopranos in the country to accompany her, I'd savor the privilege of listening to Gesù Bambino, L'Enfance du Christ, and Minuit Chretien. Each performance reached standards of world-class excellence.

Every year, she'd combine multiple choirs to perform Handel's Messiah. As I turned her musical pages, I'd watch mum achieve the extraordinary feat of conducting the choir and orchestra while simultaneously playing the piano. She'd wave one hand in the direction of sections of the choir, and bring them in at time-critical moments. There was never an error. She achieved perfection – always.

Mum was happiest on stage where her passionate spirit found its calling. As the final Hallelujah chorus of Handel's Messiah reached its crescendo, I saw her being lifted to a world far removed from ours.

My respect for mum went back to my earliest childhood days. As a five-year-old, I'd request chances to sit next to her on her piano bench where I'd sit statuesquely still so that I could absorb the purity of the sound that mum emitted. Her gift seeped deeply into my soul – and became a quality-of-life necessity.

Cadogan Drive was the reliable home bedrock upon which our whole family flourished – physically and emotionally. Mum and dad elicited each other's best qualities in beautiful gestures and small touches. Anthony soared academically at law school. He'd come home from Natal University every night and meticulously type out his lecture notes - seldom going to bed before two in the morning. Stephen was conscripted into the South African army. He fought in Angola against the South West African People's Organization (SWAPO), and made the most of a bad situation with his coping ally, a strong sense of humor. He was quick to make friends with people who required the sustenance of that quick wit.

Cadogan Drive's serenity promoted one of my life's strongest denial phases, and it played out in the choices I encouraged. I urged dad to take mum and I to one of South Africa's most picturesque beaches in the Cape – Plettenberg Bay. I was convinced that it would be mum's elixir – her rejuvenation package guideline. The plan was derailed from the start when mum grew gravely ill during our two-day car journey, and had to lie down on the back seat of our Audi for the duration of the trip. Dad and I manned the helm, taking turns driving when one of us could feel sleepiness encroach. We'd also formulated a hospital proximity plan if mum's condition deteriorated further. Dad and I were always a formidable team. I fed off his intelligent, calm gentleness, and he saw strengths in me that I didn't know I had.

When I dreaded life's cruel blows, I always put my hope in the body's redemptive ability to supersede and vanquish the thing that is destroying it. In one short month, I had already erased the memory of the phone call I took from dad six weeks earlier. As I was about to write my Bachelor's degree English test, dad called my university residence and asked someone to find me urgently. Mum had been rushed to hospital and was placed on life-support machines in intensive care unit (ICU). I told dad that I would write the English test that was critical to passing the year – and then join him at the hospital immediately afterwards. I so vividly recall walking up the long red-bricked staircase from residence up to campus – tears flooding down my cheeks. A virtual stranger walked towards me, and asked if she could help me. I said stutteringly, "My mother is dying." She put her arms around me and enveloped me in a cloak of pure human decency.

After three critical days in ICU, mum rallied, like she always did. She began to breathe again shallowly, and I rejoiced in having our mum back. Within days she'd produce her culinary coup de grâce dinners, and the strength of that effort convinced me that mum was back; nothing could prevent her from going forward. My summation was radically wrong. If I'd really seen what my head chose not to calibrate, I would have noticed that mum was operating on half her former strength.

Mum economized her residual energy by devoting it to the great love of her life - music. She listened to recordings from her friend in London, renowned pianist John Ogdon. He had often visited our home, and I had wonderful memories of being his singular audience as he practiced for recitals in our home's dining room. I watched mum as she sat in her favorite armchair, listening to Chopin's Piano Concerto No. 1 in E Minor. She'd follow that with Beethoven's Christus am Ölberge - Christ on the Mount of Olives – and I should have recognized by her listening choices that she knew what was coming, and had accepted its steely encroachment.

Mum had formed significantly close bonds with two of her music students, Julia Blanke and Janet McMartin. She loved both of them deeply. Julia was my friend, and whatever mum couldn't tell me, she told Julia. She understood my fragility more than I recognized at the time, and she mastered her bravery to save me that which I wasn't strong enough to hear. I'd walk past the music room to the sounds of Julia and mum laughing freely, and I was grateful to be part of that sound.

In Janet McMartin, mum found the perfect version of the little girl I should have been. Janet was impeccably neat and polite. She arrived at her music lessons wearing ironed buttercup yellow dresses with neat bows cinched at the waist. Her hair was always tied in a perfect ponytail with no loose strands to distract mum's sense of order. Janet followed all mum's requests diligently, and they shared a very special relationship.

My first shot of harsh reality came when I arrived home after a water polo tour. As I climbed the staircase and entered our parents' bedroom, I was forced to confront the cold, merciless truth. My talented, gorgeous mum, who was only in her fifties, was lying on her side in bed, a shriveled version of her former self. The wheelchair next to her bed confirmed my eyes' cognition. Still, the denial continued:

"Please, take it away," I blurted out to dad.

My poor dad had suffered enough, and I had to find a way to support him while urging mum to give it one last try – to will herself like she had all the times before – to fight her breathlessness and live. Yet again, she rallied – just like Maya Angelou's *And Still I Rise*.

The next day, mum asked dad and I to help her down the staircase chair lift so that she could give what I didn't know were the last of her expert lessons to her students. They were about to do their practical music exams with London's Royal Academy of Music – mum's alma mater. Despite being ashen-faced and weak, she performed this impossible feat, and after three days of intense teaching hours, she asked dad and I to help her up the stair lift again. As we ascended, she said to us, "I just gave my last music lessons."

It was in those critical few days of reckoning that I understood why I respected and revered my mother as much as I did. She was capable of transcending all worldly restrictions. Her fiercely embedded convictions gave her an all-consuming strength that transgressed the prognostic predictions of medical science.

As mum's water-clogged lungs collapsed, I called my school principal to inform him that I needed to be at home with my dying mum. Dad and I kept an all-night vigil – so committed were we to spending every living moment with mum.

Stephen loved our mum deeply, but there came a point where his pain was too immense for him to watch his mother dying. Each one of us deals with pain in our own manageable way. I understood Steve's pain intimately well. We were twins, and we'd spent nine months together in our mother's womb – awaiting our birth.

Two minutes before mum died, I told her that I loved and respected her deeply. Her last words to me were,

"Hold onto Julia." She was referring to Julia Blanke, her piano student.

Mum slipped away in the arms of dad and I at the end of those words.

Dad's grief was unfathomable. I held him tightly in the hope that he could feel my adoration for him. Mum was the absolute love of his life, and as he absorbed the magnitude of his loss, he recited the words that he and mum had always shared: "Our love is here to stay. It's very clear."

I arranged mum's funeral by choosing the best cathedral I could find that had a worthy pipe organ to honor her legacy. I called Isabella Stengel, a renowned pianist at Natal University, and before I could finish my sentence, she completed my words with,

"Of course I'll play at Lily's funeral service. Yes, yes, yes - one hundred fold yes!"

Fellow musicians are always the best critics of each other, and Isabella's volition spoke volumes. She called the best sopranos she could corral, and together, we created a program that I hope pleased mum.

Durban's Trinity Cathedral was packed to capacity as mum's coffin came down the aisle. There was standing room only, and as I sobbed in the front row listening to Isabella Stengel's performance of Mozart's *Ave Verum Corpus*, I was out-sobbed by people behind me who – like me – could not believe that this supremely gifted lady had left us so early.

I have honored mum's wishes about holding onto Julia, not because I had to, but because I wanted to. Julia Blanke-van Eden is a woman of substantial depth, and I visit her every time I go back to Cape Town. In her I find enormous comfort. We are life-long travelers, and Julia has a sacred place in the deepest recesses of my heart.

In 2014, I traveled to Switzerland – the home of Janet McMartin (now Johannsen). We met at the Lausanne train station, and the emotion in her eyes, when we ran towards each other, reflected the love she still held for mum. Many people have shared with me the generally held view that I am a splitting image of my mum. I know I have her eyes.

Janet's and my first teatime together in a Swiss hotel lounge became a liquid bath for our unstoppable tears. For the first time, I learned what it was about mum's death that broke Janet's heart so visibly when she was a child. While I had received the most beautiful, hand-written letters from Janet around the time of mum's funeral, I learned so much more in my 2014 Swiss trip. Janet provided me with a legacy about mum that I can now hold close to my broken heart. Her words are so valuable as I try to pay mum the respect that is due her.

"Mrs. Addison did not just teach me how to read music or how to play the piano. She transported me to another world. She spoke about Bach, Mozart and Beethoven like she had known them personally. She had two enormous full grand pianos in her living room (one brown and one black), and she treated them with such care. She showed me how a piano makes its sound, and the mechanics behind the different pedals. She made learning the piano look like an art form. She sold it to me. It wasn't just about banging away at scales and repeating things until they were memorized. Mrs. Addison painted a picture of a world that I found mesmerizing. I wanted to visit all the parts of the world that she represented. She made me want to be a part of her elegance. Most importantly, Mrs. Addison believed in me, even though I did not think I was a gifted musician. I loved her, and I loved everything that she taught me."

Janet's words are your well-earned homage, mum. I think you'll also be pleased to know that your beloved Bluthner grand piano will go to Janet in Switzerland one day.

As for your enormous contributions to my life: you gave me a genetic gift and an anthology of exquisite sounds that have enriched my soul immeasurably. Your music is your greatest gift to me.

Musical lesson from Mum. Anthony, Di, Steve.

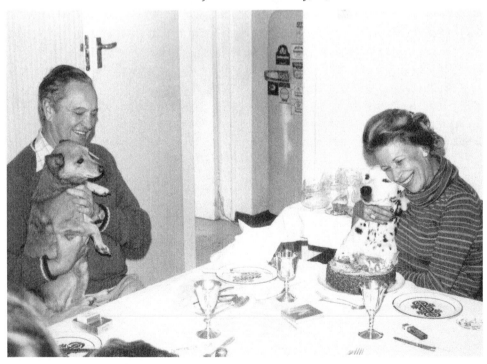

Bill and Mum with family Dalmation Clara, Cadogan Drive Durban 1980

Mum with Pushkin, Zimbabwe

Mum & Dad 25th Wedding Anniversary just before her death

Last picture of Mum, Di & Steve

Di & Julia Blanke van Eden - Cape Town 2013

Janet (McMartin) Johannsen, Di, Vicki, Ross - Lausanne, Switzerland 2014

Julia Blanke van Eden, Karen Stewart, Di, Louise Tucker, Cape Town 2018

Di and Dad - Marina da Gama, Cape Town

CHAPTER 12

Dad and Cape Town

I cannot make my days longer so I strive to make them better
-Paul Theroux

Mum's death left behind a hole the size of a planet. Our animatedly filled home became vapid, cold, bare, deathly. All the music and laughter that had sustained us - fled with mum's last breath. Her singular brilliance evaporated from every facet of our lives.

It took our first Christmas without our formidably strong matriarchal presence to realize that our world had fallen off its axis. All our attempts to do things the way mum would have done – failed wretchedly. Our first no-mother Christmas tree looked like Miss Havisham's cob-webbed mess. I invited mum and dad's friends to dinner and attempted to recreate mum's culinary masterpieces. They turned into cardboard-tasting debacles. Kylie, our Alaskan Malamute dog, moped about the house whimpering. Dad tried to cheer her up by taking her on plenty of car rides but the moment she stepped back into the house, her ears flattened. We were all desolately sad.

Dad's implosion threshold came suddenly and unexpectedly.

"I'm going to live in Britain," he announced. "I'll be leaving in a few months' time. You can stay on in the house, but it is an expensive place to run, so I advice that you rent out the bedrooms to sustain your livelihood."

Britain was not just outside the country; it was on another continent.

"Will I be able to speak to you? Do you have a home there?" I asked pathetically.

"I think I'll be living in various rentals," he answered. "I plan to travel across Europe so I won't be stationed in any location for long. No point giving you a phone number - besides, calling across the world is too expensive so you won't want to do that."

That was it! We did not hear from dad for a full two years. He disappeared to another continent to work through his grief while I became a skeletal version of my former self. I barely ate, and what little I did, I marshaled into categories and calorie-specific portions. My daily objective was to conscientiously control the residual aspects of my life that I felt were controllable.

My teaching duties at my brothers' alma mater, Northwood Boys' High School, rapidly evolved into several extra-curricular commitments. I taught English all day, and then headed out to the school's swimming pool to coach swimming and water polo in the afternoons. Our school principal, Errol Brocklehurst, was a man of enormous energy and athletic skill. He believed in me, and he strode up to me one morning and boomed,

"Lily's legacy is YOU! You've been hiding your talents under a bushel. It's time you produced all our school musical performances. I'd also like you to play the piano in the mornings for school assemblies."

I never said "no" to Mr. Brocklehurst. Within weeks I was coaching water polo at 6 am; playing the piano at school assemblies; teaching 12th grade English from 8 am – 2:30 pm, coaching swimming and water polo from 3 pm - 5 pm. School musical production rehearsals started at 6 pm, and I seldom went home before 10 pm. It did not take a genius to notice that my weight was dropping dangerously low. I was in trouble deeper than I stopped to notice.

During this time, we sold our home – Cadogan Drive. With our fragmented family scattered in various dis-connected parts of South Africa and Europe, it was collectively agreed that different lives required different roots. Our home needed to be liquidated for financial dissemination. I bought an apartment in Durban that I grew to loathe. It was a sterile, hostile environment in which anorexia took a stronghold.

After two years living abroad trying to assuage his grief, dad returned to Africa to build his post-mum nest in magnificent Cape Town. A warm sense of assuredness permeated my body as I celebrated dad's return to the country. As I fetched him from the airport, I felt elated to have my Rock of Gibraltar back in contactable distance.

Dad's substantial will to reinvent a new life manifested itself so colorfully as he relayed to me the marvelous adventures he'd enjoyed abroad. Instead of wasting money on expensive cruise ships, he'd charmed his way aboard cargo ships with his friend, American actor, Robert Mitchum. He showed me photographs of the two men engaging in each other's congenial company while breathing in the healthy ocean air.

What fascinated me most was that this was an entirely 'new dad' – one that I had never seen before. As a child, I'd always viewed my intelligent, electrical engineer father as shy; less apt to assertively engage others in conversation. How wrong I was. This was a new, gregarious dad – determined to suck out and savor all the juices of life.

While he shared the descriptions of all the new friends he'd met in different countries, I felt I was hearing American novelist Paul Theroux's *The Great Railway Bazaar* being read out loud. As if dad read my mind, he said to me that he still wished to do the Trans-Siberian Railway trip – which is a part of Theroux's *The Great Railway Bazaar.* But it was time to build a nest – temporarily.

Our life-long friends, the Whitakers, had settled in Cape Town after they left Zimbabwe. Dad wanted to be close to them - to enjoy their companionship one more time. Lesley and her husband Mark were raising their family on a busy Cape farm, and dad loved to visit them and romp amongst their animals. Dad had a great touch with furry friends. They sensed his gentle kindness, and gravitated to him naturally.

Avril Whitaker showed dad a new section of Cape Town that had recently been built. It was called Marina da Gama, and it was a similar replica of the beautiful housing developments that had gone up in Cape St. Francis. All the houses were pristine white with black roofs. Their front garden was a gorgeous marine waterway that bustled with ducks and swans. Dad fell in love with Marina da Gama instantaneously. For this waterman and strong swimmer, the environment spoke to him, and made his senses feel more alive than I had ever seen. Dad paid cash for a maintenance-free two-bedroom slice of peace. He built his own jetty and played with his small boat like a young boy discovering the joys of life.

Dad's hospitality was simple - unfettered by formalities or elaborate stages. Friends were welcome to join him on the jetty, dangling their feet in the water. He served them simple hand food – dispensing with cutlery and ceremony. He was so proud of his new life, and wanted to share friendship and stimulating conversation within the context of this serene simplicity. Our Alaskan Malamute, Kylie, joined dad in this happy environment. She'd stare out across the water at the ducks, salivating at their potential meal, while dad pottered around the garden building terraces and planting trees.

Dad wrote me so many happy letters as I continued my life in Durban. I designed him stationery with a picture drawn of him in a sled with Kylie pulling him across the nearby beach. He used his enterprising skills to find people with the same Alaskan Malamutes. He'd invite the owners with their dogs to Marina da Gama to meet Kylie, and all the dogs would frolic across the grass, enjoying a special puppy party. Dad laughed heartily with them and became his own version of an effervescent Malamute.

I developed a deep love affair with Cape Town. Its pink-hued majestic mountains and blue waters spoke to me intimately. I never grew tired of watching Table Mountain. Its colors changed with the days' moods – and as I approached it from different angles, it painted an entirely different scape. I dug my feet into the soft white sand of the Atlantic beaches while gazing at the ever-changing aqua tones of the water. Everything about this beautiful city resonated with me.

I grew to appreciate Marina da Gama as much as dad. When I'd visit him during the school summer vacations, we'd invent hilarious ways to amuse ourselves. When friends invited us to dinner across the waterway, instead of driving there, we elected to put on our bathing suits – and swim across the water to our dinner destination. We arrived wet and laughing. Our hosts provided us towels to dry off, and it became the much-talked-about Marina da Gama dinner icebreaker. Dad's imagination had no limits. He made up for every year of sadness he spent nursing mum, and I could not have rejoiced more fully for him.

During this time, I had formed a particularly close bond with Andrea Nisbet. My friend was witty, dynamic and a great horse rider. On weekends, I'd steer my car to the magnificent grounds of the Hilton College Estate in Kwa-Zulu Natal where Andrea lived in a quaint cottage. Her father, Jimmy Nisbet, was deputy principal of this distinguished school. I always spent New Year's Eve with Andrea, and we developed rituals that amused us. At precisely midnight on December 31st every year, we'd climb Hilton College's high diving board in the pitch dark, and somersault off it into the swimming pool. On weekday nights, Andrea would invite me to her little cottage for spaghetti and laughter. I'd return the favor by bringing her my almost-perfect replication of mum's macaroni cheese recipe.

The visit that I dreaded occurred on a Tuesday afternoon when a close friend, Sue Howard, arrived at my Durban home to show me the evening newspaper's front-page headlines. Andrea had been killed that day while driving her horses to a show-jumping event in Johannesburg. An oil tanker hit her in thick fog, and she burned to death from the car's explosion. I called dad immediately in Cape Town to share with him the tragic news. He wept for the second daughter he had come to love through the years, and asked me to fly down to Cape Town so we could honor Andrea's memory together with a service dedicated to her at St. James Church. I was so grateful that dad and I shared this enormous sensitivity.

Dad's need to travel and conquer new horizons surfaced once a year. During his three-month absence, Kylie would go to one of the families with Malamutes where dad believed she was completely safe. When dad returned home from his European sojourn, he went to fetch Kylie, and discovered that she was dead. The owner of her vacation home didn't know how to contact him in Europe, and only delivered the news to him at the point of her collection. He told dad that she had died underneath a tree one night. He buried her and never found out her cause of death. Dad was heart-broken. Kylie was his new-life companion; they shared trouble-free times, and I can still hear him calling her name: "Kai, Kai. Let's go. Another adventure."

As dad related his loss to me, he also briefly mentioned – like a "please pass the salt" breakfast sentence - that while he was in London, melanoma cancerous cells had gravitated fairly deeply inside his thigh, and he underwent surgery while there. My heart froze as he related the news. Dad assured me that the London doctors had caught it, cauterized the area, and that all would be well. That was my optimistic dad.

All was not well. Within weeks I learned that dad had been hospitalized at Cape Town's Groote Schuur Hospital. I made calls to gauge the severity of his condition. Bill and Avril Whitaker were in England at the time, so I had nobody in Cape Town close to the family to give me an accurate assessment of dad's situation. I didn't have dad's new friends' phone numbers either. In desperation I called a contemporary of mine, a newly graduated medical doctor who worked at Groote Schuur. This was before the time of HIPAA (Health Insurance Portability and Accountability Act of 1996) so doctors were more apt to share patient information. I asked my friend to speak to dad's doctor, and give me the nuts and bolts of what I knew I had to face.

The resident doctor's return phone call to me shut down a portion of my brain.

"The cancer has traveled," he said. "It has reached your dad's spine and he's paralyzed. I'm so sorry."

My typical speed required a new speedometer that day. Within one hour I had gone to my school principal, asked him if I could take emergency sabbatical leave, and I booked an air ticket to Cape Town that night. I skidded out of my apartment and went straight to the airport. When I landed at Cape Town International airport, Julia Blanke-van Eden's husband was waiting for me, and the next morning, I went straight to Groote Schuur Hospital.

My paralyzed dad was smiling as he greeted me, and I made a mental determination to will his body to heal – so that it could mirror his smile – catch up with his body's better state. Dad gave me the keys to his Marina da Gama home, and as I opened its front door a few hours later, I felt an unfamiliar contradiction. This was dad's happy home, a place where life was always sun-filled and perfect. As I walked into the lounge, it felt coldly austere and unwelcoming. The weather appeared to agree with my sentiment because that day, a Cape storm swept in with unabated ferocity. With hurricane-force winds whipping the house relentlessly, I feared that dad's roof would blow away with all the hopes and dreams that

Marina da Gama represented. That night I listened to Beethoven until the sun rose. It was a miserable attempt to distract my ears from the howling winds.

Dad and I made plans for the future – despite everything that was happening to his body. Once again, I put my hope in the body's ability to fight the cells that were vanquishing it. Dad had led a healthy life. Unlike mum, he never smoked; he hardly drank, and he ate healthy food groups. I didn't recall dad ever being ill before. The only time I saw him in bed during the day was when he caught chicken pox from Anthony, Stephen and I eons ago. His unshaven look was the only clue that gave away his 'not well' status. He was surely going to beat this temporary setback.

I spent the duration of every day with dad at Groote Schuur Hospital. Doctors became familiar with my constant presence and smiled at me compassionately as they saw me catching the elevator from the oncology floor. On some days, dad rallied like I knew he would. On others, he couldn't look at me.

Six weeks later, the nurse on duty called me to the hospital around midnight. She delivered the verbal blow that dad had taken a turn for the worse. As I drove dad's Mazda from Marina da Gama to the hospital, I felt that the velocity of the unrelenting rainstorm was going to lift the car right off the freeway. As my windshield wipers overworked to keep up with the quantity of water hitting the glass, I pulled off onto the side of the road like a defeated, sitting duck. In that moment of desperation I cried out for a reprieve from the inescapable forces of dread.

There was no reprieve. John Southey Addison died in my arms in the early hours of the morning. All he managed to whisper to me before passing was this unexpected certainty:

"You are going to the USA one day. It's the place for you."

Dad and I had never discussed the topic of the United States, but I unequivocally believe that when people who love us pass on, they have words of valuable wisdom to impart to us. Dad could see way beyond our earthly horizon at the hour of his death.

There were no verbal closures beyond that – no reciprocal words of comfort to each other. Morphine denied us that soothing soporific.

The world lost a thoroughly decent man – a Wits University Electrical Engineer graduate who, in many respects, was years ahead of his time. I lost my confidante, my cheerleader, and the dad whom I adored without reservation. My new orphan status felt like an imposition - something that wasn't supposed to happen so soon in my young life. Anthony and Stephen shared the same undesirable status, but more concerning, our family's life had become disparately fractured. I'll explain all of that later.

Dad cruising across the world on the Barrier Panama with friend, Robert Mitchum

American actor Robert Mitchum traveling with Dad

Kylie

Dad's Marina da Gama Home, Cape Town

Alaskan Malamute party at dad's home - Marina da Gama, Cape Town

Alexie Mcoran Campbell and Di - Zimbabwe 2013

CHAPTER 13

Roaring Twenties

It's never too late to have a happy childhood
- Tom Robbins

When the losses and complexities of life mounted, I turned to the people I trusted.

My first car was a white bullet – an Alfa Romeo bullet to be precise. This spirited little Italian car set the road map for my roaring twenties, and as I introduce you to the Mcoran Campbell family, you'll come to appreciate how they became the supersonic fuel injection to my engine.

Diana Mcoran Campbell represented the pioneering spirit of the most tenacious settlers in Africa. She grew up in Mutare, an area in the mountainous region of eastern Zimbabwe, and she married an impeccable gentleman in Ivan Mcoran Campbell. They established an idyllic home in my childhood haven, Highlands, and raised four children, three of whom were scintillating gorgeous daughters - Turia, Tinita and Alexandria.

It was not until we entered our roaring twenties that Turia, Tinita, Alexie and I became tightly bonded amigos. The electrostatic forces of attraction between us ratified all the laws of physics: each of us contributed a set of unique characteristics that formed a tightly complementary connection.

My white Italian bullet appeared to have a highly sophisticated navigational system because just as I had finished writing my last test or I'd completed grading my last paper in South Africa – the spirited señorita would drive me up to the Mcoran Campbells' Zimbabwean enclave - on autopilot. After a long journey, I'd arrive at their Newton Spicer home with loads of extra oxygen in my lungs – enough to fully engage in the exciting weeks ahead.

Diana Mcoran Campbell set the tone for all of us. The quintessential representation of the glass half full optimism, Diana found the charm in everything. Her youngest daughter, Alexie, had a Samoyed dog, and I'd walk into the kitchen to find Diana dancing around the kitchen floor with Pushkin the Samoyed. Diana's British-accented inflections added its layer of delightfulness to the scene:

"What a GORGEOUS pony you are, PUSH-KIN!" Her delivery was always very strong with conscientiously separated syllables for clarity.

At the 5 pm hour, Diana would call all of us into her bedroom. We'd lie on her bed where she'd advice us how to navigate our lives with happiness in our hearts.

"It's GREAT fun to dance. Yes, girls, you must ALWAYS take up the opportunity to DANCE." She delivered this advice while always staring at the ceiling assuredly.

When Alexie received distressing news about her boyfriend at the time, and we were all trying to find the right words to console her, in swept Diana with her resolutely strong voice.

"Now, COME along, girls. Fetch some lettuce and bananas from the kitchen. We are GOING to feed the TORTOISES!"

Incredibly, I recall Alexie wiping away her tears almost immediately. There were pets to feed, things to do. Diana kept us busy with rudimentary distractions that anchored us.

It turns out that we girls had plenty of our own distractions. As the night hour encroached, we'd prepare to take Harare by thunderstorm. One of our favorite places was Archipelago Nightclub. It was an underwater coral-coved scuba-diving expedition in dry party clothes. My senses were enthralled by Archipelago and my inner dancing dolphin came out to wave surf – musically speaking.

We sashayed across the dance floor to the music of Lionel Ritchie, Al Jarreau, George Benson, and Earth Wind and Fire. Our *Let's Groove* tonight call to sway segwayed into *Fantasy*, followed by Al Jarreau's *Mornin'* as the literal early morning hours surfaced. The all-night party was never complete without the insertion of Bob Marley into the play list. His legion of Zimbabwean devotees honored their musical hero on the dance floor with dreadlocks and Rastafarian colors. It was all so eclectic - such a colorful spectrum of humanity - and I thrived in the unifying dimension of Archipelago's musical array.

The Mcoran Campbell girls dated various eligible suitors whom they managed with confident flair. Their jet-set lives equipped them with extensive social skills that kept men interested – but slightly afraid of them. Alexie had been involved with American actor, Tony Curtis, while he was filming in London. His admiration for her was reflected in the portraits he painted, and the poems he wrote for her. That experience gave Alexie a sophistication level that few love interests could match. She attended Frank Sinatra's 60th birthday party in Knightsbridge, and she and Turia Mcoran Campbell were regular attendees at the Cannes Film Festival in southern France. Turia always caused a stir at the festival because everyone thought she was Meryl Streep.

Handsome men from lucrative oil-drilling duties in Bahrain (a sovereign state in the Persian Gulf) came home to Zimbabwe once a year, and they formed one of the many line-ups of young men seeking the girls' company. The black phone at the Mcoran Campbell house rang off the hook with suitors calling in to find out if the girls were available for nocturnal festivities.

The post war peace in Zimbabwe created opportunities for professionals from other countries to feed their adventurous appetites by journeying to this African gem. Alex Coyle, a young Scottish dentist from Edinburgh, did not just arrive in Harare - he made a Formula One entrance driving a bright red Triumph TR7. He fell in love with the Zimbabwean lifestyle – and – Alexie Mcoran Campbell. He'd speed up their Newton Spicer driveway, park it at the front door portal, and gallop inside to fetch Alexie.

Diana's Siamese cats didn't waste a moment of this opportunity. Alex's TR7 had its sports top conveniently down, so the cats decided to make a *Lady and the Tramp* movie sequel. Their *We are Siamese if You Please* song's objective wasn't aimed at milk: it was aimed at the inviting leather seats in this bright red piece of fun. In they went – digging their claws into the upholstery as destructively as suited them. As Alex emerged from the house with Alexie, and discovered his TR7's mutilated seats, he was forced to make a critical decision: blow a mental fuse over his car seats and Diana's cats - or choose Alexie. He chose Alexie.

Alex Coyle had Uri Geller capabilities. We'd all go out to dinner where he'd stare at spoons at the dinner table – and bend them with no physical touch whatsoever. Our youthful exuberance imbibed it all, and our energy accelerated with every imaginative piece of stimulation.

The entire McoranCampbell family became sought-after guests at every party. One weekend, on our journey to a farm party, Alex Coyle was driving the car when one of Africa's unrelenting storms pelted us mercilessly. Alex kept informing us about the Peugeot car's inability to cope with the rain by saying in his broad Scottish accent,

"This is a car I don't trust."

Dismissing his cautionary words, we watched him assiduously negotiating the car's wheels around six-inch mud pools. We threw our fate to the storm's winds - arriving at our destination an hour late. As we adjusted our nerves and collected our composures, Diana bounced out of the car – into the rain – saying,

"Let's walk in the rain, girls. My hair loves the rain!" Her irrepressible joy was never dampened – not even by thunderous rain.

Tinita had formed a serious relationship with Bertie Bondi around that time. He was a principled man, and both Bertie and Tinita would whisk me off to Zimbabwe's Kariba Dam for the weekend. While driving there, Bertie would tap his fingers on the car's steering wheel in timed appreciation of his extensive collection of jazz music playing. I loved it. At sunset, we'd board a Sunset Cruise boat for a tranquil float across the water. It was anything but that on one occasion. As a storm approached, the waves started whipping up against the boat as if we were out at sea. I recall my swimming skills being neutralized as I dove overboard to try to assist in anchoring the boat to the jetty. It was a force of nature that I had never experienced before.

Kariba Dam always held great memories for me because of dad's involvement in its inception phase. When the building of the dam was completed in 1960 with Kariba Gorge providing hydro electricity for the country, Africa's wildlife became victims to the flooding. *Operation Noah* was a wildlife rescue operation on the Zambezi River (on the border of Zimbabwe and Zambia) where dad contributed his valuable skills and compassion to the project.

The operation was led by courageous conservationist, Rupert Fothergill, who hoisted many terrified animals onto his own shoulders in crocodile-infested water, and moved them away from the rising flood waters. Over 6,000 animals were rescued and relocated to Matusadona National Park around Lake Kariba. Through my childhood years, as dad showed me pictures of Rupert Fothergill and he working in unison with the animals, I came to love him all the more deeply.

The Mcoran Campbells' eldest daughter, Turia, had established her main home base in Switzerland. She landed there a few years earlier because of her deep love for a man from the Geneva-based International Red Cross. He was offering critical humanitarian aid in the Rhodesian War when the civilian airplane in which he was traveling, was shot down by a surface-to-air Sam-7 missile – close to Kariba Dam. His death devastated Turia, who flew to his hometown, Saint-Sulpice in Switzerland, to comfort his family. It was there that the mutual love affair between Turia and Switzerland originated.

As we four girls approached our twenty-ninth years, we'd invested substantial time in the good-time bucket, and our all-night escapades were starting to lose their luster. My white señorita bullet had performed transportation duties to multiple Mcoran Campbell weddings, and we were ready to quieten down – to sleep more, and allow our bodies to regenerate.

By then, Turia, Tinita and Alexie were married, and I was enthused to welcome the next generation of Mcoran Campbell children into our world. I felt a personal responsibility to insure that the fun times became multi generational, so I switched my energetic hours to the daylight. The geography stayed the same. I'd drive up to Zimbabwe from South Africa, and arrive at Diana's and Ivan's home with sneakers, and enough spring in my step to carry armfuls of excited children.

"Let's explore the forest," I'd call out to them when I arrived after a two-day drive.

Kirsten, Struan and Carla were Alexie's and Turia's children, and they were clamped to my side. As we ran off into the forest with its magical trees, we'd draw sticks on who could ride on my back when their legs were tired. I bounced around with them like a monkey on steroids, and when we'd return home later in the afternoon, we'd create hiding spaces in the lounge, and use Diana's sofa cushions as forts.

Everyone needs the surety of a family, and the Mcoran Campbells were a critical family who nurtured my soul during the years of human loss. I credit them with being my North Star, and I am forever grateful for their brilliant, steadfast light.

Rupert Fothergill saving wildlife - Operation Noah, Kariba Dam

Tinita Mcoran Campbell, Jimmy Periera, Alex Coyle, Alexie Mcoran Campbell.
Our Roaring Twenties in Zimbabwe

Bertie Bondi, Tinita Mcoran Campbell, Alexie Mcoran Campbell

Alexie and Tony Curtis

Rob and Di's Wedding - Photo by Anthony McMillan

CHAPTER 14

Lyles and Liddesdale

If I get married, I want to be very married
-Audrey Hepburn

During my teaching tenure at Northwood Boys' High School, Rob Lyle headed up the history department. He was dynamic, always cheerful, and exceptionally well loved by all the teaching staff and boys. This courageous man epitomized fortitude and perseverance - under what I would soon learn - were harrowing circumstances. I had surmised that he was experiencing a challenging time in his private life, but I knew little about the severity of his trials.

I was living in Cape Town, and had just lost dad, when Rob's pulverizing tragedies peaked. His teenage daughter, Lindsay, succumbed to brain cancer after bravely fighting its ravages for thirteen months. It was a torturous loss that no parent should ever experience. Shortly after Lindsay's death, Rob's wife committed suicide. I called him immediately to see if I could help to reduce the pain in his fractured heart.

A month later, after wrapping up the vestiges of dad's life in Cape Town, I returned to Durban – determined to help Rob through his valley of inconceivable darkness. What struck me encouragingly was his capacity to find humorous moments in his darkest hours. He'd cry, laugh, and cry some more – fielding his emotions more recuperatively than I'd ever seen anybody do.

Instead of turning inwards, Rob turned outwards - volunteering to help other people. He was a *Lifeline* crisis counselor for people on the brink of suicide. He talked people off ledges with his soothing, logical approach to problem solving. He also committed to find healing for his own grief by attending well-structured meetings led by experts. Rob was superhuman.

I'd never interacted with anyone like this man. My grief in losing dad was microscopic next to Rob's magnitude of suffering.

Music amplified the empathetic basis of our friendship. Rob loved Van Halen. Their talents produced a musical sound that became a healthy conduit for his immeasurable grief. He'd turn their music up to concert-level loudness – and strut around the lounge pretending to be lead singer Sammy Hagar. I loved to see Rob immerse himself in these alter ego characters. It produced a vitality in him that became a crucial healing mechanism.

This was post apartheid South Africa, and for the first time in decades, international artists streamed back into the country for their first live concerts. Rob and I didn't waste a single opportunity. Our hearts and ears sought the power of music. After Phil Collins' concert, we bought tickets for Tina Turner's dynamic stage performance. Rob danced all over the field of King's Park Stadium in Durban – and the freedom he felt moving to Tina singing *The Best* and *Nutbush City Limits* brought down my guard – enough to allow me to acquiesce to the feelings that were already there. The rain couldn't put a dampener on this emotion. We were in love – and we let the feelings flow.

Relieved that our hearts matched, we worked speedily towards sealing our unity. Our earnest desire to start a new life-affirming chapter made us move at a pace that probably needed a speed check – but at the time it felt positively right. We were committed to jump-starting our lighter-hearted days.

Rob took me to formally meet his mother, Lynne Hayse-Gregson. She was a member of the "Old Durban" families - South African code for very posh. Since this was like a meeting at Buckingham Palace, I transformed my usual appearance by wearing a tailored suit – the type of attire I typically avoided. I also brought out my mum's pearl necklace. I greeted the smiling, impeccably elegant Mrs. Hayse-Gregson, and was immediately put at ease. She advised me that I needed to simply call her Lynne. We forged an instantly easy connection – one in which we could both completely relax.

As the African bush telegraph news spread through the Lyle family, I received a call from Bruce Lyle, Rob's younger brother. He had a law firm near the Durban dockyard, and he summoned me to a meeting at his intimidating office. My second tailored suit came out for that occasion, but when I met Bruce, I immediately recognized that he shunned unnecessary formalities. Bruce thrived on adventurous stories, humor, and extensively creative projects. He was anchored in the simple, organic pleasures of life. What stood out from the meeting was Bruce's only serious note:

"We Lyle boys are faithful to our wives, you know, Di. We don't fool around."

I believed him. His marriage to his wife, Margot, represented an exceptionally respectful union. He upheld her in all his conversations, and their actions matched their words. I knew, without reservation, that the Lyle brothers conducted themselves with the highest standards of integrity.

Rob proposed to me heartfeltly. There were no roses, no champagne – just a promise. I wore mum's engagement ring, and grew increasingly more excited as the wedding preparations gathered momentum.

Bruce and Margot's two young daughters, Stephanie and Claudia, were to be our flower girls. That part of the wedding tickled my imagination festively. I had fallen instantly in love with Stephs and Clauds - who were scrumptiously delightful. I became a child with them, and we practiced marching down the aisle to Mendelssohn's wedding march with the conscientiousness that they insisted upon. My wedding dress was masterfully made by one of my former students from Northwood School.

I was committed to a man whose value system would have won the tacit approval of my parents – had they been alive. Rob exemplified human decency. He was kind, sensitive, indescribably emotionally strong, and upliftingly positive. I never saw him wake up in a bad mood. He grasped each day with vitality and a voracious appetite for life.

We married at Rob's alma mater, Michaelhouse, in the Kwa-Zulu Natal midlands. Margaret Deeb stepped in for my mother with a level of supportiveness that was magnificent. I had spent so many healing days at the Deebs' Umhloti home after mum's death, and I shall always be grateful to Collin and Margaret Deeb for absorbing me into their lives with such generosity.

I loved every aspect about the ceremony and the magnificent school at which Rob and I married. It was reminiscent of the historically beautiful countryside schools in England with its red brick structures and sweepingly lush lawns. It promised the stable elements of history: valuable traditions, the pursuit of excellence, and the multi-generational promotion of admirable human qualities.

Rob's parents owned a beautiful piece of land in the area close to Michaelhouse known as Fort Nottingham. It was pridefully British with dark green lawn that was hydrated by the endless days of gentle mist. The Lyles' cottage on the property bore the name Liddesdale, and I grew to love our time there in increasingly satisfying increments.

On the day of our morning wedding, the sun shone spectacularly. The sky gave us its cobalt blue color, and our joy was palpable. Rob's best man, Ian, came to pick me up from the countryside hotel in which I changed. Ian shared Rob's zeal for life, so he went about dispelling all my bridal nerves by taking me for a thrillingly fast ride to the chapel. I popped my veiled head out of the sunroof, and shrieked with happiness as we raced over the rolling hills.

Bruce Lyle took me down the aisle to the sound of Michaelhouse's school song.

There was such a sense of safety with the three Lyle brothers. They were honorable men – men whose words held value. Margot had offered me her family's tiara – a privileged gesture that I greatly appreciated.

Stephanie and Claudia were the gold standard in flower girls. Claudia was unrelentingly insistent about fulfilling her duties by carrying my non-existent bridal train. When she realized there wasn't a train, she grabbed the back of my skirt anyway, and lifted it. I giggled with happiness. This was a family who knew how to take care of each other. I was a lucky girl.

I meant my vows to Rob – I truly did - and I knew I was making the right choice in husband. As we emerged from the chapel as a married couple, I wanted to swim a hundred lengths of the school's pool in celebration. We had aspirational dreams and promises of sun-filled days.

We held our reception at Granny Mouse's Country House, after which Ian lent us his sports utility vehicle so that we could make the most of our honeymoon at the family's cottage – Liddesdale. The spring blooms welcomed us with a spectacular show. The peach blossom trees were ablaze with pink flowers, and the azalea bushes gave us a striking magenta display.

With the use of the SUV, we could go up onto the area known as the commonage where wild antelope abounded. The vegetation and climate reminded me of England – less so Africa – and Rob and I spent a misty, peaceful week at Liddesdale – excited about the start of our new lives.

In the years after we were married, my new nieces, Stephanie and Claudia, gave me inestimable joy. I'd drive up to their home with its large, wild African garden, and re-activate the child in me. We'd put on pantomimes, dress up as various characters, and indulge our extensive imaginations. On Sunday afternoons all three of us would lie in Bruce's home-built hammock between two trees. I'd read to the girls in the sun, and they'd squint at me with their brains computing a magnitude of thoughts.

I'd fetch the girls to go on fishing expeditions, and we'd invent all kinds of stupid things to put at the end of our fishing rods. It was never about catching anything. It was about the experience of being out in nature next to a beautiful lake with fish eagles flying overhead. Afterwards, I'd take the girls out for an English country tea so that I could feed off their enthusiasm for life.

At Liddesdale in the winter, the Lyle family would cuddle up in front of the fireplace with our cats. In the mornings, the girls would burst into our bedroom with ecstatic joy. In the evenings, we'd choreograph dance sequences with Steph leading our trio.

Rob Lyle is an exceptional man who gave me a wonderful new lease on life. The dimensions and layers of happiness he added to my life hold an inextinguishable value.

Rob's and Di's Wedding, South Africa. Photo by Anthony McMillan

Rob and Di's wedding day, Michaelhouse, Kwa-Zulu Natal, South Africa

Stephanie, Rob, Di & Claudia

Stephanie, Bruce & Claudia Lyle

Craig, Bruce and Rob Lyle at Liddesdale

Anthony with his cat and reading friend

CHAPTER 15

Anthony and Tragedy

Silence the pianos, and with muffled drum, bring out the coffin
- W H Auden

Rob Lyle and I were newly married in the mid 1990s when Anthony was enjoying an illustrious career in London working for the multinational mining, metals and petroleum dual-listed public company, BHP Billiton's. It had a primary listing on the London Stock Exchange, and was a constituent of the FTSE 100 index. Anthony's career trajectory after graduating from Natal University with multiple degrees - was meteoric.

Anthony's resolute determination manifested itself in his toddler years. My parents relayed to me the dramatic story of how – when Stephen and I were born – Anthony struggled with the incursion of two crying babies into his almost perfect life. At age four, he set about resolving the disturbance by leaving home after his evening bath. Clad only in pajamas, he climbed onto his red tricycle, and opened our wrought-iron gates by stretching on the tip of his toes to reach the handle. Our Boxer dog, Sandy, followed him out of the gates, and as he rode down the substantial length of the road, he arrived at a busy traffic intersection with Sandy glued to his side. Our local café owner noticed this extraordinarily confident four-year-old on a tricycle, and after recognizing him as the Addison boy, he called my parents immediately.

"I'm watching your son, Mrs. Addison, about to cross Enterprise Road with a dog circling his tricycle."

Mum and dad raced down to fetch him, and apparently, Anthony didn't appear to be upset when they arrived. He was simply solving a problem his way.

In our childhood days, when Anthony attended Highlands Junior School in Harare, Zimbabwe, I recall the day when our parents were called into the school principal's office – for what they thought was a disciplinary problem with Anthony. They were pleasantly surprised to learn that the principal had called them in to discuss Anthony's I.Q test results.

"Your son is exceptionally intelligent," said the Highlands School principal. "He's in the top percentile of intelligence quotient scores."

Dad and mum promised Anthony an electric train set if he applied himself at school that year. I recall him doing the bare minimum work requirement to bring home a glowing set of school grades. My parents followed through on their promise, and Anthony, Stephen and I spent hours every day delighting our imaginations with this state-of-the-art train set.

Our family had always known that Anthony's brain fired brightly. Ever since I can remember, he was devouring an entire book in one or two days with a tabby cat nestled in his neck. He read and retained information at the speed of light. His vocabulary at the dinner table was extensive. He'd bring up the topic of "fiduciary responsibility" to our parents at age thirteen. He exercised sophisticated sarcasm long before he hit his teenager years.

When Anthony accelerated into the threshold of those years, he turned dad's workshop into a science laboratory. He'd invite Stephen and I into his white-coated lab, either to be his audience, or to conduct experiments on us – as if we were his guinea pigs. The conclusions he drew from our experimental sessions gave him the answers he needed to be three steps ahead of his school class. When his chemistry teacher set about conducting similar experiments, Anthony already had the reactionary facts tucked up his own laboratory sleeve.

One day he took it too far: he instructed Stephen to breathe in some gas – and I think Stephen passed out or he was very ill. All I remember is the commotion of my panicked parents swooping in to the workshop to find my twin in need of medical attention. Anthony didn't have a brake pedal on his curiosity. He dove into everything with all cylinders firing.

My brother's 12th grade year at high school appeared to be his breakout year. Within a few months of our arrival in South Africa, Anthony was a finalist in the National Science Olympiad™. Despite our family's traumatic first year in a new country, Anthony superseded all the odds, and his torch began to glow brightly.

My greatest regret is being too young to know how to mediate the destructive, head-on battles between mum and Anthony. Younger siblings don't have those skills. Mum's failing was her response to Anthony's precociousness. She was an authoritative disciplinarian, and her methodology of reining Anthony in by force, produced the opposite effect. The stallion bucked. Constraint was an anathema to Anthony, and so the hostility between these two passionately strong personalities festered until there was no relationship left to salvage.

By that stage, Anthony might have been studying Mahatma Gandhi for all I knew because his response to mum changed entirely. Instead of pursuing the route of raging arguments, he became passively resistant to her by exercising his right to silence. Stephen and I preferred this quieter choice because it tempered the verbal violence in our house.

I was at Natal University in residence at the time, and when I came home on the weekends, my optimistic perception of our home being a much happier place was fed in large measure by the cessation of fighting. The verbal outbursts seldom occurred, and that was a relief to Stephen's and my need for peace.

Anthony was doing exceptionally well at law school, and was productively immersed in his university curriculum – actively attaining the grades he knew he needed to meet his ambitious career goals. A skilled strategic planner, he studied the stock markets and invested money wisely.

Anthony was also in charge of our vegetable garden at the top of our Cadogan Drive property. As if he were being graded for his efforts, he'd produce fresh tomatoes, pumpkins, spinach, lettuce and carrots that rivaled the size and taste of any famous farmer. Anthony's pursuit of excellence manifested itself in every aspect of his life. He didn't just go through the motions of doing something; he excelled at it.

I loved to watch Anthony loading our two dogs, Clara and Rani, into his tiny Mr. Bean mini. He'd take them off to the beach, and they loved the creatively energizing time he spent with them. Anthony's compassionate nature was elicited most touchingly with our dogs. He'd blow sweet air kisses to Clara, and she'd smile back at him with her teeth and gums showing. After that, she'd pony prance around him. Anthony loved our dogs unreservedly, and his sensitivity towards them was returned with their all-encompassing love for him. His tough, survivalist exterior had a very tender interior heart.

I had become an assiduous observer of my family in my teenage years. I watched their faces intensely, and mentally computed their words and their actions. It contributed to the basis of a future journalistic career. My saddest study was the final, irreversible blow between mum and Anthony when I was twenty.

Mum had ordered Anthony to do something, and he passively ignored the ordinance. She ratcheted up her fury with a demand that he leave our house permanently. He pointed out to her that leaving home before his graduation from law school (at the end of that year) was not financially possible because he had no income, and his expensive, self-funded education had accrued years of debt. Mum didn't appear to hear him because she went into his closet, grabbed all his clothes, and threw them out of our second story window. When that didn't produce results, she called the police to our house to forcibly evict Anthony. Stephen and I knew that mum had gone too far on this one. It destroyed Anthony's sense of propriety. He was humiliated, indignantly angry, and I could see that it took massive restraint for him not to show his emotional response. It was impossible for me not to see it; it was written in his eyes.

The police backed off, and there was a temporary suspension of the eviction order.

Anthony stayed on in our home for three more months. On the day of his last law school test, he packed his tiny Mr. Bean mini with the few clothes he could fit inside. Clara and Rani knew that something was wrong. Animals are more sensitive than we are at understanding moods. Their beloved master didn't typically put clothes in his car, and they instinctively understood the hurt in his heart. I watched the devastatingly sad goodbye he gave them. He crouched down to their level, hugged them for a few minutes, and then let them go with a look of pain I had never seen in his face before. They stared at him with their tails between their legs. He averted looking back at them as he drove his mini down our long driveway for the last time in his life.

Anthony severed all contact with mum. He sought refuge with our cousin, Bruce Murray, in Johannesburg, and began a new life with the comfort that Bruce and Emilia provided him. They were enormously generous to my brother. In the Murrays, Anthony found stability, and the calm love that he so desperately needed.

I saw Anthony whenever he came down to Durban for the massed pipes and drums concert in our city. He was one of the country's best bagpipers, and I loved to watch him play with the rousing sounds of the open-air massed bands. We were carefully polite around each other, and after one of the concerts, Anthony specifically asked me if I was prepared to terminate my relationship with mum, so that I could come over onto his side, and join his life. I explained to him that I needed mum, and that he was asking too much of me.

When mum died that year, I called Anthony to ask him if he could fly into Durban – to make peace with her before she passed. He courteously explained that it would open up a wound that he was trying to keep sutured in place. He feared that the wound would suppurate if he saw her.

Anthony went on to conquer his dreams with speed. I respected his determination, tenacity and work ethic enormously. It was easy to be his satellite cheerleader. He was the sun and I orbited his beam with the greatest admiration.

Bruce Murray was a pivotally important mentor to him during this time.

Anthony was in his thirties with a high-flying, responsibility-laden position at BHP Billiton's headquarters in London. He was part of their acquisition team finding mining options in South America and Australia. The position was so high powered that they had their own private jet. My brother operated intensely – committing extensive hours to his career – and he had formed a tightknit group of equally high-flying friends across the world. He was not married but he was dating someone at the time.

On the day after his 40th birthday, November 12th, 1997, I received the shattering cellphone call at 2:45 pm South African time to inform me that Anthony had just jumped off the BHP Billiton's building – killing himself instantly.

My tenacious, protective older brother was a supreme survivor. His death made no sense in 1997, and it makes no sense now. He had drafted his Will the afternoon he took his life, and its contents, which spoke volumes, will remain private.

Anthony and Stephen altar boys. Nazareth House, Zimbabwe

Anthony (top row 2nd from right) Highlands School, Harare 1969

Mum & Anthony 1959

Di and Stephen pulling Anthony out of the pool – Lake Chivero

Anthony (kneeling front center) law school graduation night 1982

Anthony - Final Year - 1997

Anthony – 1997

Bruce Murray with Rob Lyle

CHAPTER 16

Leaving Africa

If I know a song of Africa, of the giraffe and the African new moon lying on her back, does Africa know a song of me?
- Isak Dinesen

I n my mid thirties, I did an inventory check on the mounting deaths in our family. In 36 years I had lost three of my four nuclear family members. Suicide, in particular, is a devastating death form. It leaves behind pervasive, rhetorical questions that can never be answered. I lay awake at night imagining the sense of abject desperation Anthony must have felt in that fatal moment. He was capable of conquering all life's obstacles, and it made no sense that he would have imploded.

Our cousin, Bruce Murray, carried his own post-suicide pain. A natural leader, he had taken Anthony caringly under his wing and mentored him like a big brother. At Anthony's funeral at Trinity Cathedral, Durban, the same cathedral where we'd held mum's funeral, Bruce kept saying, "what has this boy done; what has this boy done." Bruce and I sought each other for comfort. Together, we were determined to find healing by utilizing the palliative power of humorous anecdotes while sharing stories about Anthony's highly-charged life.

Nelson Mandela was in power in South Africa with his magnanimous leadership. Two years before Anthony's death, I had left teaching to open up a training company, *Addison and Associates*, to bring about a solution phase to the damage that apartheid had left behind. It had denied the African people a dignified place in the South African economy, and I recognized that tens of thousands of aspiring citizens needed skills training to enter the corporate world. One of my university majors was Industrial Psychology, and it proved to be an effective tool in devising training programs for people entering the field of supervisory positions, in particular.

I felt a sense of contributory usefulness to the new South African dawn. My favorite assignments were going out into the rural areas to guide the 12th grade African teachers. Their educational system was severely compromised, and I was determined to share with them some of the keys towards fast-tracking their students to more hopeful tomorrows. I loved the work.

My home province of Kwa-Zulu Natal had other complex problems post apartheid. The Zulu tribe, who predominated, clashed with the minority Xhosa tribe over long-standing grievances. It produced its own cauldron of violence that was severe enough to warrant Nelson Mandela intervening as an emergency mediator. We all realized that had it not been for Mandela's superb leadership, the conflict could have erupted into a full-blown war.

The issue I was about to confront, though, was a land grievance issue, and it further escalated the violence in an already deeply divided province. It was exacerbated by the scars left behind after apartheid where most black children had been raised without parental guidance. Apartheid had forced millions of black adults to seek work in white-only areas. They couldn't bring their children with them, so they left them behind with grandparents in the rural areas or townships. Those children received little education, and grew up in conditions that would create massive societal problems later. There were increasingly agitated demands to reclaim land that had previously belonged to South Africa's indigenous people – and to re-distribute it amongst the impoverished people. Criminal elements climbed into the genuine grievance base, and produced an era of dangerous violence in the province.

I was working for a forestry company in an area called Richmond in Kwa-Zulu Natal. It required me driving out to the area and staying there for the entire week. As I went about booking my accommodation in what looked like a beautiful lakeside area with individual cottages, the owners of the lakeside bed and breakfast asked me if I was traveling alone, and if I was armed. I didn't possess a firearm and even if I did, I wouldn't want to use it. When they learned this, they advised that I not stay at the cottages because there had been some incidents. They gave me no more detail than that. Put simply, it was not safe for me to stay there. Instead, they gave me the phone number of a local farmer whose property was equipped with the latest high-tech security protection. They advised me to contact him. I did, and the farmer offered me one of the rooms in his farmhouse. I accepted the offer. When I think back, it was fairly risky to accept accommodation in a complete stranger's home when I knew nothing about him.

I arrived at the farm on a Sunday afternoon. The farmer had ominously instructed me to make it in during the daylight hours with the implication that nighttime travel was not safe. As I pulled up to his huge electrical gates, I honked my car's horn to signal my arrival. The farmer would not give me any gate codes, of course, and when he heard me, he opened the gates from his remote controls in the house. During those short few minutes, I had already performed a detailed inspection of the environment.

All the fencing around the huge property had high voltage electrical wires with signs everywhere saying "Danger. Don't touch." The next part was wholly unexpected. The farmer's seven Boerboel Mastiff dogs approached my car intimidatingly with no happy dog tails wagging. This breed of dog is prolific on South African farms and their express purpose is not to be friendly. They are trained to fiercely and aggressively protect the farmer's property with their powerful, muscular bodies – and a bite force potential of 800 psi.

Despite my knowledge of the breed, I made the mistake of opening the car door, and just as I stood up to stretch my legs after the long drive, the farmer yelled towards me from his kitchen door.

"Freeze! Don't move. Don't look at the dogs. Wait for me."

He walked towards me - armed with a semi-automatic weapon strapped to his side, and he commanded his seven dogs to move to his heels. They obeyed him instantly.

"Wow. You have loyal dogs," I remarked stupidly.

"Come with me," he commanded. "If you walk with me calmly, the dogs will know that we are friends. If you separate from me, they'll attack you."

My new farmer friend spoke with a strong Afrikaans language accent, and as I surveyed his physical presence, I noticed that he looked exactly like his dogs. He was massive, muscular, hairy and intimidating. I gulped. This was going to be an interesting week.

I retired early to bed that night in the hopes that the drama would recede – but it intensified.

"Don't fall asleep too hard," the farmer warned.

"The army will be performing a reconnaissance check on us around midnight tonight. It's for our safety. The reason for this precaution is that our next-door-farm neighbors were tortured and murdered six weeks ago. The men who did it are still at large, and there is some concern that they are targeting my farm. The security forces come in here every night to make sure that we are not tied up. It also helps if the attackers know that they don't have the whole night to operate. Tomorrow morning, I will escort you to your car. My advice is for you to leave for work at different times of the day so that the people who are watching us don't see a familiar pattern. We must be unpredictable."

I was in the hands of a farmer who had mastered the art of mitigating the daily risks that besieged his life, and I followed his precautions diligently in a methodical, sensible manner. But I do recall that week being a watershed phase of my life. For the first time, I became an anxious driver. I'd furtively look at my rear-view mirrors all the time while I was traveling between the farm and the forestry training facility.

My brain was on investigative overload as I tried to recognize faces I had seen the previous day; familiar car license plates; anything suspiciously unusual in the people following me on the road. I wrestled uncomfortably with the idea of purchasing a firearm for future training trips in this area. Had my work been mainly in the city, I would not have worried, but the reality was that the majority of Rob's and my livelihood lay in rural hot-beds with their attendant risks.

Anthony and Richmond were the two catalysts behind the significant changes I made in 1998. I decided to spend three months in London - teaching in the British high school systems. Rob could join me later on, and earn valuable pound sterling currency after he'd completed the South African school year.

I jetted off to London, and rented out a room in Primrose Hill – a beautiful part of the city with Regent's Park nestled perfectly in its midst. I loved the area with its architectural history, and the dark green park became my valuable exercise valve.

My enthusiasm was dramatically tempered the next day when I met my school students for the first time. I had to catch three underground trains to find the school - and when I walked into the equivalent of a 10th grade classroom, the behavior I encountered was a disturbing jolt.

The teenagers in this school didn't want an education. They followed Pink Floyd's *Another Brick in the Wall* anthem in all its self-defeating purposelessness. They'd shout out nonsensical sentences to me that illustrated how desperately they needed an education. These were lost, angry souls, and I wasn't prepared for the insurrection. It was Blackboard Jungle only for those brave enough to navigate the assault.

The situation was compounded in the following weeks by the onset of the cold-to-the-bone damp English winter. I had one radiator heater in my apartment, and this obsolete piece of equipment took hours to warm itself. I'd come home from school frigidly cold from the rain that pelted me sideways as I walked the mile from the train station to the apartment. My body wasn't used to these conditions, and my blood certainly wasn't thick enough.

I'd spend pathetic evenings trying to dry my clothes on the radiator while performing one of those cartoonish running rat scenes with my heat-seeking hands pitter-pattering along the top of the radiator. My diet was equally as sparse. I'd crunch on toast while opening up chemically infused cans of tomato soup.

Humor became my coping mechanism as I struggled with the complex teenagers of London's Elephant and Castle district. There was a reason my services were needed in the area: the existent teachers couldn't cope with the angry students, and either they'd ask to be transferred out of the district or they called in sick because the environment wore down their resilience.

On Friday nights, I'd join a supportive group of teachers from New Zealand and Australia, and we'd laugh away the week's troubles at our favorite place, *The Long Island Iced Tea Café* in Leicester Square. I'm not a proponent of authoritarian education. With its attendant use of corporal punishment, I've seen its damaging effects in Africa. I am, however, a firm believer in the advantages of classroom environments where mutual respect is the established premise. Respect is an essential component of the educative process.

Beyond the challenges of teaching teenagers whose problems prohibited an education, I reveled in the rich depths of London's history. Each Sunday, my faith was fed by services at Westminster Abbey and St. Paul's Cathedral. The music at both esteemed churches was auditory bliss, and the sustenance of that weekly experience lifted my spirit. Christmas Eve service at Westminster Abbey holds a particularly special place in my heart.

When Rob eventually flew in to join me, I was excited to greet him at Heathrow Airport. He was surprised to find me with laryngitis, a hacking cough, and I was still recovering from the stabbing incident I had witnessed in my school's playground a few days earlier.

One of the girls in my class decided it was a constructive idea to bring a sharp instrument into school so that she could stab one of her classmates at recess. I don't know how she smuggled the weapon past security but she succeeded.

I was on duty in the school's playground at recess, and I witnessed the girl use full force to drive the instrument into her victim's head. As I ran towards both of them, I watched in slow motion how the blood squirted profusely from the boy's head. We called an ambulance immediately to rush him to hospital, and after that, I had to put in a police report. I recall commenting to the school principal that I wasn't sure I had the characteristics to meet the requirements of the job. Its education title was a misnomer. Poor Rob was about to walk into his own baptism of fire, and he responded with as much shock as I did.

I had been given a particularly tough assignment in Elephant and Castle where the fractious problems of poverty and alcoholism spilled into the classroom. Not all schools were like this. On one particular week, I was assigned to a school where the students' lives appeared to be less chaotic, and the behavior was quantifiably better. Interestingly, I was also assigned to a school of Islamic Pakistani immigrants where there was absolute silence in class. As I taught the group through the week, I began to recognize the complexities within their silence. They were stoically reserved – and averse to any interaction with the teacher. The tenor of distrust presented its own set of educative dilemmas.

In the middle of London's winter, Rob's cousins invited us to spend a week in California, and we jumped at the opportunity to feel the warmth of the sun again. As we took off from Heathrow Airport on a Virgin Atlantic flight, I remembered dad's words to me – "The USA is the place for you". We landed in palm-treed Los Angeles where I felt an instant sense of easy belonging. I imagined what a fish must feel like when it finds its way back to water – and this was the sense I had.

After Rob and I visited a Beverly Hills immigration attorney, we were informed that we met the specialized skills entry requirements into the USA. The wheels turned rapidly as the American doors opened. Rob and I returned to South Africa - resolved to sell our home, and make plans for a future on the other end of the world. There were so many considerations, and as we negotiated the variables, it became clear that the changes would impact Rob and his eighteen-year-old son the most. I sensed Rob becoming more anxious as we discussed departure dates. He had far more to lose than I; he was invested in a school with a substantial pension awaiting him if he rode out the longevity of his career there.

To his considerable credit, Rob continued to encourage me to lead the way. He advised me to proceed ahead of him; to set up a home base in California so that he and his son, Chris, could join me later.

I've analyzed why my resolve to leave Africa was so emphatically strong. At Anthony's funeral, a relative walked up to me and said, "There's a curse on the Addison family." My hope was that if I moved ten thousand miles away, the curse would elect to stay in Africa, and not follow me to my new life.

There was much more, however, behind the decision. Every time I drove past our Cadogan Drive home, I became incorrigibly sad. I could never call a place a home when it felt like a burial yard. I wanted to close the chapter of sadness, and move to a continent where people's life expectancies in the 21st century made reaching 59th birthdays reasonably possible without death's intrusion.

Stephen had also had enough. He left South Africa and immigrated to Australia where he began a new life. When pain is deeply ingrained, changing the geography of the emotional spillage is often the perceived solution.

The value of solid friendships became inestimably clear to me in the months leading up to my departure from Africa. Megan Donnelly Bell had become my closest, most reliable friend since my mid twenties. In Megan I found a trustworthy confidante, and a solid human keel who caught me when the winds threatened to topple my sails. When dad died, Megan was there. When Anthony died, Megan was there. Her family took me in as if I were a member of their nuclear core. Megan showed me that no matter what life threw us, we could always work through it together.

When I conveyed the heart-searing news to her that Rob and I were going to move to California, she championed our decision. Not once did Megan show me that my departure would leave behind a massive void in her African life. She rallied for me and stood by me.

The day before I left Africa, I drove up to Bruce Murray's home to hand over Mark II of Anthony's Mr. Bean mini. Leaving that behind, and driving away from Bruce was one of the hardest farewells I've ever experienced. Bruce had been a pillar-of-strength cousin and big brother to me. We shared hilariously energetic times in the Drakensberg Mountains of Kwa-Zulu Natal, the cottage at Liddesdale, and Michaelhouse rugby games. I knew I would miss him terribly.

Rob and Megan took me out to the airport. I said goodbye to Rob with a great deal of hope in my heart because he promised to see me soon. Megan turned and ran as I went through the security gates. She knew she wouldn't see me for years, and the sadness that squeezed her heart was massive. I felt a flood of emotions, and within that context, I also had a curiously uplifting feeling: Megan was six months pregnant with her only child, Téa, and as I boarded the airplane to Los Angeles, I already knew that this baby girl was going to play a significantly special role in my life – even with the transcontinental distance.

Di and Megan, Franschhoek, South Africa - 2016

Anthony's Mr. Bean Mini

Megan and Di – Franschhoek 2016

Di in California - Photo by Curtis Dahl

CHAPTER 17

California Dreaming

Made up my mind to make a new start, going to California
with an aching in my heart
- Going to California – Led Zeppelin

C alifornia resonated with me palpably. I landed at Los Angeles International Airport, and never looked back. My cousins, Brian and Wendy Gregson, absorbed me into their Californian life with unwavering physical and emotional support. They also gave me the gift of their rescue dog, Lucy, who found a way into my heart from the inception, and filled a hole that I didn't know needed filling. The Gregsons' generosity to me has been infinite.

Beyond that, I knew that the buck stopped with me. I had to light my American career fire immediately while navigating the complex legal immigration system. Anybody who believes that the legal immigration route here is seamless needs a reality check. Despite meeting all the merit-based entry qualifications into the USA, I discovered that it was a massively complex process involving avaricious, expensive attorneys.

The daunting challenges ahead in the USA were softened at the inception by the power of human kindness. All the warnings I'd been given by some South African friends about the endemic superficiality of Californians were disproved before I'd even unpacked. The first thing I needed to do was pass my Californian driver's license test. While standing in line at the Department of Motor Vehicles (DMV), I saw a striking blonde behind me who came to my aid as I struggled with the vernacular of the DMV clerk. Her name was Deanné.

"You look like a girl who is in need of a cup of tea," she proposed supportively.

Deanné gave me far more than tea. She went on to provide years of supportive, massively generous friendship.

Deanné - the dolphin - from Malibu was my first official American friend. I was so uplifted by this first milestone that I planted a flag on the front lawn with a sign: Found First Friend.

The following week, on a cold winter's day, Deanné took me kayaking off Malibu's Latigo Canyon. We paddled out in her double kayak wearing Pacific-Ocean-proof wetsuits, and formed a bonding sisterhood in the tangling masses of kelp. The wonderful aspect about kayaking is that it invites partnership and supportive cooperation, particularly as I learned about the currents of this new ocean. Deanné shared her heart and her knowledge with me, and I absorbed all her gifts with alacrity.

What followed can only be described as miraculous – beyond any human manufacturing. Deanné had met a special person in Israel while on vacation. They'd exchanged phone numbers, and that person happened to live in my neighborhood of Westlake Village outside Los Angeles. I received a phone call – inviting me to spend Thanksgiving dinner in the home of this generous-hearted stranger whom I'd never met.

On Thanksgiving Thursday, I arrived at the front door of a house that spoke of warmth and love. As I walked through the open door, the first person I encountered was Bob Eubanks. I didn't recognize him because all his successes had never been broadcast in South Africa. I met my gracious host, Deborah, but was pathetically confused about who belonged to which person - maritally. As we all engaged in conversation, I tried to reduce the confusion.

"So, Bob: how do you fit in here?"

"I'm the gardener," he replied with an emphatic face. I was impressed with the standard of gardening, and continued to put my foot into my mouth.

Of course he wasn't the gardener! He was THE Bob Eubanks, the husband of THE Deborah James – whom I'd later call Deborah Zebra during another life-affirming experience that I'll describe later.

Bob and Deb forgave me for my crassly stupid introduction, and that is a testament to their senses of humor and their enormous kindness. As our friendship germinated and blossomed under the balmy warmth of the Californian sun, Bob and Deb were my backbone, the cheering squad and the sureties whenever challenges surfaced. Each of their strengths contributed masts to my yacht – so that I could sail forward and onward through the currents.

Bob and Deb's son, Noah Eubanks, was born in 2003, and as I held the one-hour-old Master Eubanks in my arms, he transformed me – made me a better human being. The love I felt for this little baby was absolute, and I'd come to find out just how absolute in the coming months.

As Deb drove her SUV in our neighborhood, I was with her in the car and chatting amicably when, unexpectedly, Noah had an unusual meltdown. We tried to console him but when he wasn't responding to any of our attempts, my spring-loaded new instincts made me involuntarily somersault over the front seat into the backseat to reach Noah. All Deb saw was my derrière flipping over as she was pulling the car off onto the side of the road. The somersault turned out to be utterly useless; within sixty seconds, Deb retrieved Noah from his car seat, and burritoed him. He stopped crying immediately. That traveling scene will remain in my memory treasure-trove – always.

When Noah was eighteen months old, he'd run towards me with his arms outstretched. When I'd join the Eubanks for dinners out on the town, Noah and I would disappear underneath the tablecloth, playing all kinds of fantastical games in our private cave. In the summer months, while he rode on my back in the swimming pool, we'd play submarines and sharks. Submarines meant underwater submersion; sharks meant gliding above the water while singing the *Jaws* theme tune.

In 2006, when the Californian wildfires ravaged everything in their path with terrifying flames threatening to destroy the Eubanks' home, I ran up the steep street towards their house, yelling from the driveway, "Give me Noah!" Crises paint our priorities in clear, bold clarity.

I had been freelancing for various magazines internationally ever since my English teaching days. When I was a teenager, luxurious Sunday afternoons involved lying by the swimming pool reading the latest *Vanity Fair*, *Cosmopolitan* or *Harper's Bazaar* magazines. Their glossy covers and their content captivated me. I'd pore over them for hours – assimilating the structure and objective of each magazine.

The reason I had immigrated to the USA in 1999 was that I saw the American Dream in all its enterprising glory, and it was evident in every component of Californian life. I loved its infinite potential and the observable success stories around me. The United States encourages vision; it rewards talent that is energy-driven, and optimism is a central feature in American life. Instead of saying "no", Americans say "yes", or "let's think about this. How can we make this work?" It was so different from my own experiences in London or South Africa.

It took some coaxing and a few rational conversations with my cousins, Brian and Wendy Gregson, for me to recognize that doing other magazines' cleaning-up-work was not a viable, long-term proposition. In 2009, Brian and Wendy did the right thing by throwing me off the cliff – proverbially – giving me no backdoor to change my mind on starting *Westlake Malibu Lifestyle* Magazine. They ferried me in their family van to the computer store, and assured me that they'd made the decision on my behalf. Their confidence in my capabilities has always been an unflinching boost, and it has given me much strength through the years.

Westlake Malibu Lifestyle became my passion. The writing flowed easily, and the interviews with celebrities, athletes and heroes piqued my interest. Each interaction with the myriad of exceptionally talented people I've met since 2009 has stimulated me colossally.

I shall always be grateful for the opportunity to spend the day at Dustin Hoffman's home. He welcomed me with warmth, humor and humility. We took turns playing his beautiful Steinway grand piano, and as I left his home, he said to me,

"Promise me that you'll go back to the piano seriously one day."

I nodded and smiled in appreciation of Dustin's gentle encouragement. I intend to keep my promise.

My life appeared to come full circle when I interviewed Gregory Peck's family. He had won an Oscar award for his sensitive performance as Atticus Finch in *To Kill a Mockingbird.* During my South African teaching days, I'd taught this classical book to legions of students, and my interview with Gregory's daughter, Cecilia, gave me valuable insights into the author, Harper Lee, after whom Gregory's grandson is named. Cecilia and I enjoyed substantial conversations on Gregory's interpretation of Atticus Finch, and the graciousness of the family gene pool became evident in the answers they gave to my complex questions.

It's difficult to single out highlights in my magazine career because there have been so many non-comparable but equally valuable stories.

My meeting with Priscilla Presley produced an exceptional conversation once we transgressed this question:

"Is this going to be an interview about Elvis or me?"

"There'll be one question about Elvis, and everything else is about you," I confirmed.

Priscilla and I talked for hours about the justices and injustices of the world. We shared a mutual love of animals, and if only time weren't such a valuable commodity, we would have chatted for hours more.

Given my literary interest in Ernest Hemingway, I greatly appreciated interviewing Mariel Hemingway. Her capacity to be raw and vulnerable in discussing her family's mental health challenges gave the rest of the human race permission to admit their vulnerability.

Interviewing Robert Wagner at his Beverly Hills home brought about its own special moments. He and Natalie Wood had married within the same year as my parents, and I grew up watching *Hart to Hart* on television in Africa. I found him to be genuinely sincere and refreshingly unguarded. He wanted to talk about the special people and places in his life.

Just before the 2012 Olympics, the cover shoot and story of multiple gold medalist Greg Louganis (the world's greatest diver) impacted me greatly. He described how at the 1988 Seoul Olympics, he had been diagnosed with HIV six months prior to the Games, and given the prejudices and stigmas that abounded, he recognized that if South Korea discovered this, they might have banned his entrance. He faced indescribably difficult challenges once he arrived in Seoul including hitting his head on the diving board while performing. I recalled watching the incident on television, and as I recoiled in sympathy, Greg went off to have five stitches inserted into his head. Despite suffering concussion, he came back within the hour to dive again – and win a gold medal. It was one of the greatest acts of courage I had ever witnessed. Greg and I chatted about the incident, and he described it as his greatest Olympic moment.

Recently, I was enjoying Harry Connick Jr.'s concert at the Hollywood Bowl. His three daughters joined him on stage, and I saw something unique in his middle daughter. I followed my instincts and within a few weeks, we were doing the cover shoot for Kate Connick. That's what I thrive on – the idea generation - and the speed towards the fruition of a goal.

I've also loved the process of resurrecting the careers of famous models that were told – once they hit 28 years of age – that they were too old for the industry. With the support of my IconicFocus Models NYC/LA sisterhood in New York, and Lori Modugno in particular, we've sought to right that wrong by reinvigorating the models' careers. Beauty, or our perceptions of it, has no age limit. Models have to be representative of all sectors of society.

Some of the models with whom we work have survived traumatic situations in which abuse became a systemic pattern in their lives. They've done the work needed to break the pattern, and emerged far stronger people. Others have created charitable organizations that are moving mountains combating violence in society. Swedish/American model Jill Sorensen is a perfect example of a courageous woman who is so effectively helping the victims of domestic violence. Her *Knock Out Abuse* platform has changed countless lives for the better.

Productive collaborations have often followed many meetings. After I had interviewed Kelly Emberg and Ruby Stewart for one of our cover stories, Kelly joined our magazine as a features editor. Apart from her writing skills, she's a dynamic person who is engagingly positive. As time has evolved, all the right people have fitted into place organically - contributing their talents to my passion project.

My gratitude to Brian and Wendy Gregson, Deanné and Everett Rollins, Bob and Deborah Eubanks, Karen Lanfear, Terry and Lori Schroeder, Russell and Karin Argue, and Christopher and Theresa Parkening, is immense. They have absorbed me into their family lives, and shown me the qualities of superb friendship.

Rob Lyle made the decision – once I had immersed myself in a career in Los Angeles – not to leave South Africa. I respected his decision, and retreated after I found out that there were complications. It never detracted from my overall summation of him as one of the best human beings I was fortunate enough to have in my life. Rob encouraged me to pursue my American Dream with vigor. He promised me that he would be the first person to raise the flag if I succeeded – and I was deeply appreciative of that. He married a friend of ours after my departure from Africa, and I continue to wish them happiness in their lives.

California met more than my dreams. This warm state gave me roots upon which I could build the Goldilocks and the Three Bears Chapter II phase of my life. Dad was right. The USA was the right place for me, and California brought out the squeaking baby dolphin in me.

Di swimming off Hawaiian coast - 2011

Di, Rachel Hunter. Westlake Malibu Magazine 2015. Photo by Curtis Dahl

Deanné and Everett Rollins

Karin Argue, Anke Magnussen, Tracey, Ampa and Didi (Gawler family)

Wendy Gregson, Lucy and Di

Noah Eubanks with Deborah

Shaun Tomson, Sean & Russell Argue

Spanish Guitarist Pablo Sáinz Villegas and Di. Parkening International Guitar Competition. Pepperdine University, Malibu 2018. Photo by Ron Hall.

Deborah James, Karen Lanfear & Di - California 2019

Jimmy Connors & Di, Lake Sherwood California. Photo- Curtis Dahl

Dustin and Lisa Hoffman Westlake Malibu Cover. Photo by Andrew McPherson

Catherine and Prince William - California 2011. Getty Images

Mariel Hemingway. Westlake Malibu Magazine. Photo by David Paul & Getty Images

Priscilla Presley Westlake Malibu Cover. Photo by Chris Ameruoso

Olympic Gold Medalists Greg Louganis, Julianne McNamara,
Maurice Greene and Will Simpson. Photo by Curtis Dahl

Cecilia Peck & Ondine Peck-Voll Westlake Malibu Cover. Photo by Curtis Dahl

Kim Alexis & Di - Tilley Andalusians California. Photo by Curtis Dahl

Kelly Emberg, Ruby Stewart Westlake Malibu. Photo by Curtis Dahl

Susan Holmes-McKagan Westlake Malibu Cover 2018. IconicFocus Models NYC/LA. Photo by Patrick Xiong

Duchess Catherine and Prince William at Santa Barbara Polo 2011. Photo by 2MC Studios

Prince William playing horse polo at Santa Barbara Polo Club 2011. Photo by 2MC Studios

Anke's famous breeding stallion, Cortilo, on his 24th birthday

CHAPTER 18

Horses and Royal Oaks Farm

*A horse gallops with his lungs, perseveres with his heart,
and wins with his character*
-Tesio

Africa's large stretches of open savanna create the open canopy in which sufficient light can reach the ground to sustain the growth of large tracts of grassland. Those endless grassland tracts feed the massive herds of wild animals on the continent. While most people I know love ocean views – I love savanna views. They evoke for me the warmest feelings from childhood.

Attaining my USA green card took eight long years. I spent that valuable time working as a Training Manager for a large Los Angeles corporation, and my immersion there honed new skills and a greater understanding of the American market.

During that time, I spent a Saturday with Dr. Richard Stevens, a renowned horse veterinarian in California. I wanted to investigate the intricacies of his daily routine, and the ailments that beset horses.

He took me to *Royal Oaks Farm*, and only later would I come to appreciate how Dr. Stevens' routine visit was about to enhance the quality of my Californian life substantially. As we drove up the long driveway of the farm, I stared at the vast open savanna with its occasional trees for horse shade. The strong, multi-colored horses on the property looked like an oil painting with the moving portion of their swishing tails set against the backdrop of our clear blue skies. The sight spoke to my senses, and enthralled the inner child in me.

I was introduced to *Royal Oaks Farm's* Anke Magnussen, a dynamic force of nature. This dignified lady commanded respect with her rock-solid presence, and the strength of her voice. Her immense love of life, and her dedication to her horses were apparent in the first minute of our meeting. She smiled with her eyes, and as they sparkled, she said,

"What are you doing at 5 o'clock this afternoon? You must come for a glass of wine."

It was impossible to say no to Anke Magnussen. Why would I? I wanted to feed off her enormous energy, and join her world of infinite possibilities. As we sipped our wine while watching the horses across the savanna grassland, I felt one of the greatest senses of peace. My heart yearned to be a part of this environment.

We sat on our Adirondack chairs enjoying the softness of a gentle breeze that was caressing the tops of the golden grass. It was in that first meeting that I came to know how Anke had come out from Germany to start a new life in the USA. She earned the immediate respect of horse experts with her specialty breed, the northern German Holsteiner breed. This large, warm-blooded horse dates back to the thirteenth century, and it excels in high-level equestrian events such as dressage and show jumping.

As the months ensued, I came to acknowledge that Anke was the unofficial ambassador of the district. When new neighbors arrived on nearby farms, Anke reached out her generous hand, and invited them all to dinner so that they could establish the support groups that horse owners and land stewards needed.

When people from other countries visited *Royal Oaks Farm*, Anke organized dinner parties in her comfortable cottage so that they could feel integrated – less alone. I often looked at the people seated around her dinner table, and on some occasions, there were up to eight different nationalities represented at one table. I re-named her dinner parties the United Nations because Anke brought people together harmoniously, and gave them a friendship platform to discuss their cultural differences. More importantly, she helped us all understand that we have far more similarities than differences, and that we are all bonded as a human family. As Anke presided at the head of her table on each dinner occasion, she raised a toast to the horses that brought everyone together.

This highly disciplined, exacting lady created for me a visionary world. Will Simpson, a humble, exceptionally good-natured gentleman, rides at *Royal Oaks Farm*, and considers himself Anke's brother. In 2008, he quietly went off to the Beijing Olympics and won a coveted gold medal as part of the United States team in show jumping. Will was the last rider in a team of four, and his brilliant, flawless round on a feisty horse produced a euphoric response amongst the USA spectators in the Hong Kong stadium.

We wanted to welcome Will back to our special part of California, so the neighbors and Anke led the charge. They erected a huge banner and placed it high over the road between two roadside trees. It read, *Welcome Home Our Olympic Gold Medalist Will Simpson*. Anke sent a chauffeured, official-looking black SUV with an American flag to Los Angeles International Airport to fetch Will. Celebrities who lived in the neighborhood pulled up in Lamborghinis to celebrate the great homecoming of Will Simpson. It represented everything I had come to know and love about Anke's world: the efforts everybody made were gargantuan; the imaginative possibilities knew no limits, and the generosity of spirit flowed without constraint.

One of Anke's celebrity neighbors went on the Dave Letterman Show and expressed his relief at purchasing his new property in the same area as one of the most seasoned party lovers he'd ever met. He simply referred to her as Anke – in the same way that Oprah is just Oprah; Beyoncé is just Beyoncé. Everybody knows Anke. When you arrive in Europe, somebody at the gathering knows Anke. When you land in New York and mention Anke, somebody shrieks, "I know her!"

Anke's fame goes beyond her extensive knowledge and care of horses. Her 12-cylinder AMG Mercedes-Benz has a power base that matches her energy, and being a passenger in her car is not for the faint-hearted. Her German Shepherd cross wolf, Romeo, travels in the front seat next to her, and the security personnel at guard-gated communities hear the roar of her engine approaching, see Romeo sitting proudly in the front, and they open the gates reverently.

In 2016, I purchased my Californian home with its ideal architecture. My small garden feels adequate because I have *Royal Oaks Farm* as my large-African-acreage outlet. The quality of life that I can access just eight miles up the road from my home provides a perfect lifestyle balance.

The most important characteristic that I respect in Anke is her irrepressibility. Whether the moments are history making or not, she ignites the world around her, shows up, and enhances the quality of everyone's life. She celebrates every day like nobody I have ever met. *Royal Oaks Farm* is a hope-charged, celebratory haven with an extra infusion of catalytically positive energy.

Anke Magnussen, Will Simpson, Ty Simpson

Anke with Contefino on his birthday

Will Simpson wins the gold medal at the Beijing 2008 Olympics

Jamie Foxx welcomes Will Simpson home after the 2008 Beijing Olympics

2012 Olympic Men's Water Polo Team with Terry Schroeder, center, and Di, bottom row. Photo by Curtis Dahl

CHAPTER 19

USA Water Polo and an African Safari

To uncover your true potential you must first know your own limits, and then you have to have the courage to blow past them
- Picabo Street – Olympic Gold Medalist

2012 was a landmark year. My USA citizenship was granted after I'd finished bulleting the answers I had learned on American history to my examining officer. The supreme elation I felt - as the examiner announced that I was officially a U.S. citizen - manifested itself in the girlish sprint that carried me involuntarily through the building and out into the sunlight. Wendy Gregson shared the elation with me, and as she drove me home, Bob Eubanks was the first person I called so that I could thank him for steering me to the right attorney.

I had struggled for over twelve years to attain my American citizenship. The impact of finally achieving what I often feared would be an impossible dream – was immeasurable relief. That night, Brian and Wendy Gregson had Westlake High School's band come to their house to play me the *Star Spangled Banner*, after which they treated me to a dinner in which American flags and apple pie abounded. As I let the apple pie melt on my tongue, I thought about dad. This was his celebration too. Brian and Wendy gave me license to indulge all my energy in the stratospheric realm in which I flew. As I ran around as if it were my sixth birthday party, they laughed alongside me, and gave me more balloons and flying equipment than my parents ever gave me in childhood.

Within five months of attaining that citizenship, another dreamlike chapter of my life evolved. Before the 2008 Beijing Olympics, I had met Terry Schroeder at an international water polo game. I still loved the game, and never missed an opportunity to watch a riveting performance between the USA and one of the eastern European countries, particularly. The 2008 USA Olympic Men's Water Polo team was led by head coach, Terry Schroeder, who contributed his legendary skills towards the team's ascent to the gold medal final against Hungary. I did much of the local press coverage for the team, and the silver medal they brought home from Beijing was an honorable feat. They came home to a heroes welcome.

Four years later, Terry took virtually the same team to the 2012 London Olympics. The objective was to retain a tried-and-tested successful veteran squad in the hopes that the collective experience would serve them well and douse their nerves. It's always a concern at Olympic level that younger players, while having great fitness levels, may not be able to cope with the mental pressure.

I committed to joining the Schroeder family at the 2012 London Olympics. I'd come to know and like many of the players, and it felt right to be there, supporting them fully. Moreover, I'd formed close and trusting friendships with Terry, Lori, Leanna and Sheridan, so I looked forward to spending time with a family who had been extraordinarily caring towards me.

After working all night to put *Westlake Malibu Lifestyle* to press, Wendy and puppy-dog Lucy drove me to Los Angeles International Airport to catch my flight to Heathrow.

This was my first return to London since Anthony's death, and I grappled with conflicting emotions during the night's flight. My childhood Zimbabwean friend, Alexie Mcoran Campbell, fetched me from the airport with her son, Struan, the little guy whom I used to carry on my back during our adventurous days in Harare. Now in his twenties, he had grown into a strappingly handsome man and a consummate gentleman. Alexie and I finished each other's sentences, and couldn't wait to luxuriate in having each other's exclusive company for a full ten days. We had sixteen years of news to bring up to speed while also reminiscing about the joyful exploits of our roaring twenties.

The next day, as I caught three trains to the Olympic stadium on the opposite end of London, I did a 360-degree mental adjustment so that I could be sensitive to the mental dynamics the athletes and coaches were experiencing.

The beauty and tragedy about the Olympics is that it produces feelings of indescribable ecstasy or heart-stabbing pain. The lofty expectations of the USA Men's Water Polo team – both back home and internationally - had become a psychological disadvantage. They had everything to lose if the scoreboard didn't match the expectations. Conversely, when nothing is expected of a team, they play freely - unencumbered by nervous restraints because they have nothing to lose.

Despite the psychological pressure, Terry's team began their first week with the power and control that had defined their play leading up to the Olympics. With three wins already in the bag, there was a tangible sense of podium possibility. They had reason to retain their optimism and hope. Another medal was in sight – if only the pendulum kept swinging in the right direction.

Revenge is a powerful weapon. In the 2008 Beijing Olympics, Serbia had lost to the USA men's team in their semi-final game. The loss stung them badly because they'd presumptively notched up a victory before they'd even played. Four years later, they dove into the pool – determined to reverse the humiliation by trouncing team USA even if it cost them their lives.

Their volitional tactic worked. The USA lost to a Serbian team that played like it was their last match on earth. Judicious refereeing is always a sore analysis in water polo, but the damage had already been effected. A few days later, Croatia, who would go on to win the gold medal at the 2012 Games, defeated the USA, and the loss felt like a leg amputation. Lori, Leanna and Sheridan Schroeder formed a protective membrane around Terry while I shared theirs and the whole team's grief.

London held many emotions, not least of which was my walk through the area where Anthony lived and thrived before his tragic death. We passed his home unavoidably along our route to USA House, and as I walked back to the train station late at night - I became subdued and reflective.

Those lonely, late night train rides were generally my Achilles heel – but on one particular night – the ride evolved into something comfortingly special. I encountered an exceptionally good person who read my fear when I'd missed the last operational train of the night. Together, we caught an historical London black cab, and my new acquaintance insured that I was taken right up to my front door in the early hours of the morning. He expected nothing in return. Acts of kindness like that are enormously encouraging.

That one act of kindness begot another the next day. Brent Wiltshire, my former student from the school wherein I'd taught in South Africa, texted me while we were having dinner in London. He began investigating the possibility of the USA Men's Water Polo team coming out to South Africa – to play against their South African side. Terry and the team requested an African Safari thrown into the mix – and I received an immediate response from Brent: The answer was an affirmative YES!

As I flew home with the team after the Olympic Closing Ceremony, their mood matched the ravaging effects I was experiencing from a head concussion. One of the team's most powerful players had accidentally hit me on the head with the water polo ball, and as we took off from Heathrow, the sweating, disorientation and nausea associated with head concussions assaulted me. The team and I shared our worst plane ride ever.

I've learned through life that when we experience our deepest pain, there are promises of restorative tomorrows. Terry and the team were in deep pain after London, but in just six months' time, they were going to visit a continent they'd never seen, and go on a wild African Safari. The trip was intended to heal, to thrill, and to gain another valuable perspective on life.

The African 2013 trip was my first return to the continent of my birth in fourteen years. I had kept away deliberately until my U.S. citizenship was safely achieved, but also because I wasn't sure I was brave enough to face Africa and leave it - on my own. This opportunity gave me cushioning and padding – enough to shield me from an emotional journey that would invoke complex memories.

There was another huge dimension to this trip. My closest friend in South Africa, Megan, had given birth to Téa Bell in 2000. Sensibly, Megan and her husband waited to see if Téa and I were going to gravitate towards each other naturally. When Téa was barely a two-year-old toddler, she confidently climbed on the phone to me, and chatted away with a vocabulary that was music to my ears. Without any prodding from her parents, she had already painted a picture of her fairy Godmother in America. At Christmas time, she'd gather her cousins conspiratorially into the kitchen, and whisper to them,

"I have a fairy Godmother in California! Sshhh. It's a secret."

When Téa turned three, Megan officially asked me if I would assume Godmother duties to her daughter. For the first time in Téa's thirteen years, I was finally going to connect with her, and spend four valuable weeks discovering all the significant aspects about her that had eclipsed me. As I conscientiously prepared for our meeting, I seriously debated whether to arrive in Cape Town wearing fairy Godmother wings and a white gown. In light of Téa's teenage years, I figured that she would be utterly mortified if I did that.

After the Schroeder family, the team and I checked into our Cape Town hotel in preparation for the water polo game against South Africa the next day, I went out to dinner in Camp Bay's, and just as I settled into my chair, Megan, Gordon and Téa crept up behind me, and placed their hands gently on my shoulders. It was one of life's greatest moments to turn around and hug Téa for the first time. She was gorgeously perfect. The child I had loved ten thousand miles away for thirteen years was finally touchable – visible – and within the orbit of my heartbeat.

South Africans are an adventurous group, and nothing animates them more than a smart team joke. I received a phone call in my hotel room the day before we were due to play water polo against South Africa, inviting the team to visit Ernie

Els Wines in the picturesque Stellenbosch wine region. Ernie Els is a four-time major golf champion. He was also runner-up in the Masters Golf Tournament in 2000 and 2004.

"The invitation is a personal one from Mr. Ernie Els himself," said the caller, "and he looks forward to seeing all of you tomorrow morning at his vineyard."

In one minute I was onto them: they were planning to render our team paralytically drunk before the afternoon game! I declined the tactic with a request for another date.

The next morning, our group faced a critically serious extortion incident that tested our nerves severely. Criminal minds are nefariously cruel, and they leave behind trails of destructive consequences. The responsibility for the incident's outcome rested on my shoulders, and my central nervous system went into overdrive as I set about resolving it. I've always been a proponent of acting swiftly, and it worked in this case because we flushed out the South African individual who had made false allegations against one of our players – in an attempt to extort money. The incident gave our group a burning lesson on the importance of sticking closely together, and having each other's backs covered.

As we arrived at our afternoon water polo game against South Africa, Brent Wiltshire and our South African hosts gave us a welcome that was all-consuming. Our team, including Terry Schroeder, who played for the first time in many years, beat the South Africans in a televised game that was good-natured and full of humorous anecdotes. The party that Brent organized afterwards provided the beginning phases of the incremental healing process. This was the first time some of the team members had seen each other since the London Olympics, and they were able to completely exhale with laughter and friendship nourishing their bonds. The addition of water polo players from previous Olympics was also a great additive to the congenial mix.

A very special dimension of our trip was about to be recorded for perpetuity - courtesy of the brilliant Californian photographer, Curtis Dahl. He and his wife, Bren, accompanied us with their skills, generosity of heart, and exuberant energy.

After a short airplane ride, our group arrived at Shamwari Game Reserve in South Africa's eastern Cape district. Despite inclement weather, the photographic safari graduated into a spectacularly special experience with our first morning resembling an action-packed movie.

As the sun rose shyly behind the aggregating cumulus clouds, we took up our positions in four indestructible all-wheel-drive jeeps. Our knowledgeable game rangers communicated with each other on their two-way radios that a large pride of lions had just brought down a massive kudu antelope. Our leaders at the jeeps' helms responded immediately – careening over rugged terrain – at times levitating the vehicles to speed up their descent into the action-packed scene.

We played the part of supportive passengers by assisting the game rangers against any lawsuits by ducking if we saw head-banging tree branches coming our way. There was collective laughter ringing out from every jeep as we hit rivulets that sprayed water all over us. We notched it up to an exhilarating day in a medium in which we felt completely at home.

As we approached the lions, I will never forget the sense of fulfillment I experienced as I watched the elation on the faces of all my American friends. This was their first visit to the African wilds. More dramatically, this was the first lion kill they'd ever experienced. They were enthralled, and as I surveyed the uniquely visible emotion in each facial expression, I felt that my mission was accomplished. I had shared so viscerally with them the intimate secrets of a continent that I loved deeply.

Téa sat right next to me, and I vividly recall that it was her moments of silence that penetrated my heart the most. It's in the quiet stillness of life that we are given the gift of discovery. All we have to do is read the eyes that tell a thousand emotions.

After the alpha male lion fed sufficiently, the lionesses lined up for their feeding frenzy. Their fiercely powerful paws swatted any pride member who interfered with their access to the kudu carcass. Their brutal viciousness reflected their voracious appetites and the 'survival of the fittest' truism in the harsh African bush. My adrenalin surged every time the low guttural growl of the lions permeated the air. I'm fairly certain that everybody else must have been feeling the same surge.

An hour later, our game ranger, Anthony, took a controversial risk – one that could have ended badly. In an earnest attempt to give Curtis a *National Geographic* photographic opportunity, he instructed him to follow him – and the two men walked cautiously towards two young male lions that were walking across a wide piece of savanna. Our main concern was the mother lion that was watching her two sons avidly from a nearby hill. An attack may well have come from her. As Curtis lay down in the grass to take photographs that were truly magnificent, his wife was in significant need of a double shot of the strongest alcohol on the market. It was nerve-racking to witness the live action unfold with the unpredictability that makes the African wild so intoxicatingly exciting.

Our African Safari was drenched in sensorial moments. At night, our hosts broke out into song, and rendered beautiful renditions of *Nkosi Sikel' iAfrika* - the national anthem of South Africa - in four-part perfect harmony. They danced rhythmically as they sang, and we joined them in a human train that spoke of unity and appreciation.

The Schroeder family and I extended our trip to go up to Marataba Safari Lodge near the Zimbabwean border. All my childhood memories permeated my senses as we traveled through terrain that I knew intimately well. The trees were all nostalgically familiar, and when I saw our first troop of baboons, I dissolved into the hilarious laughter they'd always evoked from me.

Baboons are highly mischievous creatures – always concocting tricks on each other. They perform endless rituals too. They de-flea each other's bodies; massage each other's heads, and show deference to the huge alpha male. He, in turn, behaves braggadociously, flaunting his power around all his female subjects. The baby baboons – particularly the young males – will often chance their luck with their big daddy by pulling his tail, and he retaliates by smacking them. I've watched it happen so often, and the amusement effect never fails on me.

A particular highlight at Marataba was 'Twitch', the name we gave to a magnificently large, black-maned lion. His face was scarred from all the territorial fighting he'd done through the years, and this resulted in the severance of some of his facial nerves. It gave him an unwanted, involuntary twitch that obviously didn't affect his popularity with the lionesses. He had two equally magnificent females on either side of him.

What I found most fascinating was watching how a supreme alpha lion like Twitch would find the alpha equivalent in a different species. He stared at Terry fixatedly – as if Terry was going to steal one of his lionesses. We have the pictures to prove the discomfort he felt at being in the presence of a fellow alpha male.

After bidding my American friends farewell in South Africa, I flew into Zimbabwe to both reminisce about the past, and confront its present-day reality. My reunion with the Mcoran Campbell family was the trip's highlight, and the time I spent with Lydia Kafulani, the matriarchal angel from my childhood, was priceless.

But I was deeply troubled at President Robert Mugabe's tyrannical rule over the land, and the fear that he'd invoked in his people was morally reprehensible. African dictatorships are often the continent's entrenched response to fears that democracy will cause their over-throwal – their violent deaths. It's an unforgivable mistake - one that causes terrible suffering amongst the people I have loved lifelong.

After a farewell dinner with Gordon, Megan and Téa, I faced the inevitably painful departure back to the United States. Bonds that are significantly meaningful carry the weight of traumatic airport farewells. We soften it by always saying *Au Revoir* –until we meet next time.

Dr. Terry Schroeder at the Beijing 2008 Olympics as Head Coach. The team made it into the Gold Medal final against Hungary - to take the Silver Medal

Visit back to Nazareth House, Zimbabwe. Mum's Messiah performances were here. Di - 2013

Di playing piano - Vergelegen, South Africa 2013

Alexie and Di. London Olympics 2012

USA and South Africa line up for the anthems. Photo by Curtis Dahl

USA's Ryan Bailey vs South Africa, Cape Town 2013. Photo by Curtis Dahl

South Africans converge on Terry Schroeder - USA vs South Africa, Cape Town 2013. Photo by Curtis Dahl

USA Olympic Men's Water Polo enjoying relaxation time in Cape Town. Photo by Curtis Dahl

*Megan, Di, Téa & Gordon - USA vs South Africa Water Polo,
Cape Town, South Africa. Photo by Curtis Dahl*

*Di with former student Brent Wiltshire - the organizer of the USA vs. South Africa Game in
Cape Town, South Africa. Photo by Curtis Dahl*

Brent Wiltshire's hospitality in Constantia, Cape Town. Photo by Curtis Dahl

Alpha Lion "Twitch" at Marataba Safari Lodge - 2013

Lori & Terry Schroeder, Di, CapeTown 2013. Photo by Curtis Dahl

Giraffe at Shamwari Game Reserve - 2013. Photo by Curtis Dahl

2 young male lions photographed by Curtis Dahl

Anthony with Curtis Dahl - photograhing the two male lions

Di & Megan dancing with staff at Shamwari Game Reserve, South Africa 2013. Photo by Curtis Dahl

Game Ranger Anthony driving us at Shamwari Game Reserve - Schroeders, Dahls and Di happy to be drenched in the wet action. Photo by Curtis Dahl

The Baileys and Schumachers shark cage diving - Cape Town 2013. Photo by Curtis Dahl

Leopard, Madikwe Safari Lodge 2014

Lori & Sheridan Schroeder, Di - Africa 2014

Sheridan Schroeder and Di - California 2015

Téa & Megan - Franschhoek Cottage South Africa 2016

Megan,Téa and Di - Cape Town 2016

Turia and Di - Gstaad, Switzerland 2014

CHAPTER 20

Serenity and Switzerland

500 years of democracy and peace
-Graham Greene

A broken heart transported me to Switzerland in 2014. My lifelong Zimbabwean friend, Turia Mcoran Campbell, lives in a piece of earthly heaven - La Tour-de-Peilz. It's a small city pertly perched on a gentle hillside overlooking Lake Geneva, a pristinely clean lake fed by melting snow from the Swiss Alps.

Seeking the protective comfort of Turia was instinctual. Ever since childhood, she had always represented integrity, surety, reliability and purity of heart. She was also great fun - just like her mama. The musical inflections of Turia's voice always stimulated me, made me lean forward so I could appreciate each carefully delivered syllable.

My arrival at Geneva Airport could not have come soon enough. I'd already gone through immigration and customs screening at Zürich Airport. When I landed in Geneva, and retrieved my luggage from the carousel, I assumed that there had to be more layers of security screening. As I searched for those layers, I was rescued by the voice I'd been longing to hear:

"Di! Here! I'm here. *Ici!*"

It was the glorious sound of Turia's voice. I fell into her embrace instantly, and absorbed the enveloping sense of safety that being in her presence provided. Just like in our roaring twenties, we skidded out of Geneva airport with vigor and purpose: there were places to see, things to do, and life to live!

There were so many healthy dimensions to our lifelong friendship: we'd bask quietly for hours, musing and gently sharing our thoughts - and then we'd fire away with great bursts of energy.

At Turia's home that night, I crawled into bed purring like a leopard cat. I was six thousand miles away from the source of my broken heart, and Switzerland's Matterhorn was calling. As I disappeared underneath the comforter, I had one of life's best sleeps.

The next morning, the distant sound of the morning train awoke me, and I jumped out of bed like an exuberant tourist. Turia's and my first day was spent along the shores of Lake Geneva. We climbed the rocks along the water's edge, and sat in the chairs next to the large fork in the lake, which is a landmark for the Nestlé museum.

From there we took a relaxing, meandering walk down to Montreux, my favorite town. It's nestled in a palm tree-fringed microclimate with year-round moderate temperatures. It's also home to the famous Montreux Jazz Festival – where legends are born. Every summer, the two-week festival draws enormously talented musicians to its shores. Aretha Franklin, Ella Fitzgerald, Marvin Gaye, David Bowie, Elton John and Stevie Wonder have all gathered here. David Bowie and Freddie Mercury came to live and work in the region. Prince, and Deep Purple, helped to write the legend of the place in their songs. But it's Deep Purple's story, in particular, that tickled my imagination.

As Turia and I sipped cocktails on a hotel balcony overlooking the setting sun on Lake Geneva, we recounted the story of Deep Purple being there when Montreux's casino burned down. As it happened, they wrote their number one hit song, *Smoke on the Water*. I imagined the billowing white smoke channeling its way across the water – the same idyllic place at which we were gazing. It gave me a sense of being in Deep Purple's main artery – feeling the throbbing beat of *Smoke on the Water* that very night.

The next day we ventured up into the Swiss Alps to Gstaad. It involved two train rides – the scenic one being the GoldenPass Line with the glass roof. The Swiss chalets set against the backdrop of lush-green steep mountain passes were enchanting. Most importantly, Turia and I were able to take long walks on verdant pastures that invited us to have those deeply satisfying conversations.

Lori Schroeder and her sister, Robin Harman, joined us from the USA a few weeks later. Together we took boat rides across the lake, rode up trains into the Alps, and when Turia was able to join us, we ventured across the water into France. We frolicked across vineyards in silly outfits, and drank water from the crystal-clear water fountains that channeled the purest, thirst-quenching Alps snowmelt we'd ever sipped. At midnight, we'd walk through the streets of La Tour-de-Peilz in matching red pajamas. Everything about the trip was exactly what I needed. I was in the company of caring friends who transported me to a place where laughing from the stomach again – returned naturally.

In 2015, Turia joined Lori, Robin and I in Lake Como, Italy, and later on that week, we crossed the border from Northern Italy into Switzerland – this time to St. Moritz. Our taxi ride en route gave us a ride up mountain passes with some of the most exquisite scenery we'd ever seen. Fields of plump, winter-coated horses grazed on green carpets of grass that was punctuated by the first flurries of white snow. Lori, Robin and I ran around in the fields at the base of the mountains, and laughed like uninhibited children.

In 2017, I went back to Switzerland – this time to the gorgeous home Turia had built with a magnificent view over Lake Geneva. Turia had two bicycles securely locked in her garage, and on this trip, we cycled everywhere. Turia worked at Clinique La Prairie - the most beautiful work environment I'd ever seen. It is situated right on Lake Geneva, and with my increasing confidence and independence around the area, I'd pack a nutritious lunch for Turia and I, and join her by riding my bicycle down the charming little streets that eventually coursed their way to the Clinique.

When Turia finished work at 5 pm, we'd sit out at quaint restaurants overlooking the lake, and watch the sun cast a red streak across the water as it prepared to set. When we were perfectly satiated - ready to sleep - we'd ride home in the clean night air.

On the weekends, Turia and I would catch the funicular up to mountaintop homes that were built centuries ago. We'd walk through the grounds, marveling at the life that people must have enjoyed from this viewpoint. When we felt like a bite to eat, we'd stop at tiny mountaintop restaurants that were often converted flower stalls made of stone. Their low, wood-beamed ceilings required head ducking as we entered. It all served to add quaint ambience to our experience.

Apart from the truly breathtaking beauty of the country, what Switzerland represents for me is solidity, stability and a sensible balance between modernity and time-honored traditions. It is free of political arguments at dinner tables, posturing or extravagant shows of wealth. It is very un-Swiss to be ostentatious. There are no presidents in motorcades, and whoever is in office, maintains a very low-key presence. The current president of the Swiss

Confederation for 2020 is Simonetta Sommaruga – and she has very limited power. Frankly, nobody gives a toss about the lady. There are 26 cantons in Switzerland, and each one is a sovereign state with its own borders.

Turia is the human extension of what draws me to Switzerland. Her value system is steeped in family and lifelong friendships. She leads an honorable life, and enjoys the simple, nature-bonded pleasures of our humanity. Our Sunday afternoons are spent walking in the nearby forests, picking walnuts off the ground, and lying down on the forest's floor so that we can inhale the densely oxygenated air.

The adult lives that Turia and I lead on separate continents are vastly different from our Zimbabwean roots. We've acknowledged, through a lifetime of experience, that genuine contentment lies in simplifying our lives; in respecting our natural environment enough to not destroy it for our own selfish gain. Each of us is profoundly appreciative of the quality of the Chapter II lives we've created in our respective countries, and our reunions are enriched by the expanses of our life experiences.

Di playing piano in Switzerland - 2014

Di, Lori, Turia

Letting go of past hurts - Lori, Terry, Sheridan and Di - 2016

Di, Robin and Lori - St. Moritz, Switzerland 2015

Di, Robin & Lori - Switzerland

Di, Turia, Lori & Robin - France

Turia Mcoran Campbell & Di - Lake Geneva Switzerland 2017

Turia - Lake Geneva - 2017

Turia Mcoran Campbell - Switzerland 2017

Di, Turia, Montreux, Switzerland, 2014

Jordan, Olivia, Georgia, Jeremy and Annette Nel and Di -
1st Safari Night, Madikwe 2018

CHAPTER 21

USA and Africa Full Circle

If we do not do something to prevent it, Africa's animals will be lost to our world, and her children forever
-Nelson Mandela

T he Eubanks family assimilated me into their lives wholeheartedly the year I landed on American shores. Their son, Noah, became the son I always wanted, so when Deborah asked me if I could take she and Noah on their first African Safari, the significance of the request infused my senses deeply. April 2018 was our planned takeoff, and I implored the clocks of time to skip six months of the year so that we could board our flights before my anticipatory cheeks burst.

Two families joined us on the expedition: the Moores from California, and the Nels from Cape Town. Deb and Noah Eubanks landed in Johannesburg via London while the Moores came in via Zürich. In the morning, we all levitated out of our beds fast enough to be waiting in the hotel's front lobby an hour before the arrival of our Safari bus. When it FINALLY arrived, we boarded it with new definitions of avidity, and set off towards Botswana.

I had twelve Bart Simpson children in the bus with me. Every ten minutes, the song rang out reliably:

"Are we there yet?"

I smiled. My friends were about to appreciate that African time has its unique bush clock where the hands only respond to sunrise and sunset.

In the golden afternoon hour, we arrived at Madikwe Safari Lodge, a huge track of untamed land that accommodates the technical border between

Botswana and South Africa. As we drove into the massive poacher-protected, electric-gated animal sanctuary, my American friends' reaction to our first zebra sighting was a promising start to a journey I hoped would impact them for perpetuity.

After the initial scream of, "Look at the Z-E-B-R-A!" the teenagers scrambled over each other's bodies to gain the best vantage point at the left-sided window. I giggled with happiness. This is how it was meant to be. My childhood memories of Africa were merging with their new memories – forming a united coalition that we could share and treasure for its life-well-spent value. Noah added the best touch by re-naming his mother - Deborah Zebra. That was it! From that day forward she would always be Deborah Zebra to me.

Our first Safari escapade in our brawny jeeps was just before sunset – the propitiously appropriate time as everyone was adjusting to Africa's sunrise sunset clock. The Nel family, who were waiting for us at the lodge, formed the vital supplementary components to our group's 180-degree perfection. This beautiful, highly accomplished family added an inconceivably complementary dimension to our group. Their collective family height made them taller than the elephants and giraffe, and as we all bobbed around in the bumpy jeep, I glided into my at-peace space. The wind caressing my face and blowing through my hair was the physical confirmation that I was home – back where it had all started. Mum, who had worn her cat-eyed sunglasses in Hwange, was gone, but I was carrying on her legacy with my about-to-be-stolen blue aviator sunglasses pointing into the horizon.

Our first sighting was a massive old bull elephant. I recall how much he impacted Brenda Epperson Moore, who took pictures to remind her of how he had touched her soul. I went right back to Anthony's, Stephen's and my first bull elephant sighting in Hwange where mum had to perform the fastest reverse-gear escape drive over ant-hills. Back then, our bull elephant was angry and wanted us to be gone. This old man – despite his alert 90-degree-angled ears – tolerated our presence with the wisdom of his age.

Deborah Zebra and I shared a passion for giraffe. As our jeep respectfully approached a herd of them, we followed the undulations of their graceful necks until they raised us to the fluffiness of their two-horn-pronged heads. We mused in awe at the soft liquidity of their eyes, the usefulness of their long eyelashes. There are no mistakes in nature. Everything has a purpose, a use.

The next morning, the puffy, white cumulonimbus clouds quenched the red earth with a gentle rain shower, and politely cleared in time for our morning safari drive. I stayed behind on the patio of my round, thatched-roof chalet to enjoy the morning matinee of multiple monkey weddings – in the same way that I had watched them in my Highlands-tree-house childhood. Lots of ebullient, white-faced Vervet monkeys did Olympic-gold-medal acrobatic routines on the tree branches. I loved watching them in their natural element – so different from the frustrated, chained-up monkey that bit Anthony and I in Beira all those years ago.

As different emotions enveloped me, I was reminded so powerfully of the goodness in the African people. Rebekkah, one of Madikwe's employees, came to my chalet in the middle of the night to insure that I was safe. She selflessly deprived herself of a good night's sleep to keep her African sister company. We shared stories about life, our hopes, dreams, disappointments and triumphs. She walked half a mile down the road from the kitchen the next morning to bring me a nutritious tray of breakfast. Those touches of human kindness – human sensitivity – are indescribably restorative. I shall never forget the magnitude of Rebekkah's heart.

Three days later, we traveled to one of my all-time-favorite wild animal reserves, Marataba Safari Lodge near the Zimbabwean border. Bart Simpson's "are we there yet" song accompanied us amusingly on this cross-country venture. I exhaled deeply as we approached the familiar vegetation that was inculcated into every fiber of my being. Just as I'd hoped, my American friends fell as deeply in love with Marataba Safari Lodge as I had - years ago. Its nuanced charm was visible in every carefully curated detail. The massive, luxury tents carried a careful balance between that raw African feel, and enough sturdy, man-made features to keep out marauding lions.

It was already nightfall when we pulled up to the electrical gates, and because of precautionary measures with elephants, particularly the protective matriarchs, all of us had to disembark from the bus, and climb into waiting jeeps. Just that simple transfer gave us an undeniable thrill. We were in the animals' territory and we had to obey their rules - not ours.

Our first night safari racked up a ten-out-of-five-star rating. Earlier in the day, Terry Moore was so elevated by safari fever that he'd gone exploring – away from our tents and into territory that invited investigation. It all appeared to be relatively safe until our night of reckoning.

Our game ranger informed us that he had heard from the African trackers that a large male lion had moved into the area. All of us were united in our unflinching determination to find this elusive big boy. As our two jeeps ploughed through off-road terrain, the scratches they incurred from the thorny acacia tree branches reminded us that our unrelenting quest was taking a toll on the vehicles. None of us regretted the decision.

Twenty minutes later, Terry picked up the earth-moving vibration of a lion's roar. We circled the area repeatedly, switched off the jeeps' engines – waited – held our breaths – nothing. We circled again as if we'd determined that finding this lion would change the course of our lives – irrevocably. It did more than that.

In the dark recesses of this African night, we began to see a massive, black-maned lion emerging from the foliage that had completely hidden him during all our circling efforts. He had just finished mating with a female lion, and he was giving his body a ten-minute break before the next cub-making piece of action.

We froze into the centers of our two converging jeeps. Deborah mouthed to me, "Is this PG-13?"

"It certainly isn't," I whispered back without moving anything but my mouth muscle.

I assisted our game ranger by shining a powerful infrared light onto the male. Never in my substantial life had I seen a male lion this large and this magnificent. His length must surely have broken all lion records for size. His temporary satiation away from the female became our safari highlight moment. He walked right towards us – forming his own alpha male assessment of whether we presented a threat.

The thrill intensified as we watched the lioness stand up and move away – towards another massive black-maned lion who was chunkier – more muscled than his rival. I had never witnessed a lioness playing up two males as wantonly as she did. She used both of them for her survival-of-the-species copulation advantage – and I was mightily impressed by the size and supremely healthy condition of both dads. Interestingly, when a lioness gives birth to her cubs, the same litter can have different fathers. It's a cub survival mechanism against infanticide because each male who has mated with the lioness believes that the cubs belong to him. He won't kill cubs that he thinks are his.

After observing the three lions' hot-and-heavy night of passion for about thirty minutes, we respectfully withdrew from the area so that they could pursue their pleasures without an audience. As we arrived back at our lodge, it occurred to me that Terry had been walking without any protection a few hours earlier in the area in which the three lions were mating. It was a startling realization, and therein lies the thrill of Africa. There are risks, adrenalin-charging adventures, and moments of heart-pounding excitement that make us feel more alive than we've ever felt.

I had just experienced the most thrilling safari night of my life. As I lay in my tent in the early hours of the African morning, I kept hearing the vibrational earth-moving roar of the two male lions we had just seen. The sound commanded respect and invoked my deepest appreciation of the African lion's place in the animal kingdom.

The privileges of seeing so many sights that people wait a lifetime to see – continued unabated into our final day at Marataba. Just after sunrise, we saw two lion cubs hiding under a bush with their mothers. While the adults slept, the cubs spat at us with as much ferocity as they could muster.

Having all learned that African time revolves around sunrise and sunset - we set out at the twilight hour when the lighting on the great Waterberg mountain range is golden pink. The jeep we'd come to know and trust transported us safely over the lip of a gushing waterfall with Deborah and Noah sitting tightly next to me.

We watched an old elephant – an nzou yakura – looking slightly drunk as he swayed on three legs while feeding on his favorite acacia tree. Trusting our intentions, he allowed us to move in closely. We saw our first pair of rhinoceros thudding the earth's surface with their heavy-weighted bodies. A lonely male ostrich did a mating dance in front of the confused rhinoceros pair while we lamented the sad state of the ostrich's affairs. Our game ranger informed us that lions had killed the rest of the ostrich family, and this poor bird was the sole survivor. We wondered if we could assist him with an ostrich-dating app.

Just as we were wallowing in the satiation of our good fortune, our jeep turned the corner and slowly approached two young male lions that were basking in the warmth of the red earth. Just as we thought that our cups couldn't runneth over any more, three more lions emerged from some foliage and gave us an up-close-and-personal view into their courting rituals. The female was precociously loaded with hormones, and as she roared coquettishy at the two incoming males, she'd crouch, then smack the males with her huge paw. They were afraid of her; this was way too much confrontation for their burgeoning adulthood, and they made it clear that they weren't ready for her advances.

The final treat that night was our jeep's descent into hippo territory. The most deaths in Africa are caused by hippo that respond aggressively to anyone getting in their way as they try to access a water hole. Noah really wanted to see his first hippo, so our game ranger complied by taking us into water-straddling bulrush country. As the night's temperatures dipped, we became colder in our open jeep. Noah solved the problem by producing body heat. He sandwiched Deborah and I while promising to always keep us safe. It was a moment of gold-weighted significance – one that I will hold onto lifelong.

As I boarded my flight back to the USA at Oliver Tambo Airport in Johannesburg, I re-lived how it had all started.

Anthony, Stephen and I were born in Zimbabwe to John and Lily Addison. Our first wildlife adventure was with the charging bull elephant at Hwange. That night, while lying in bed in our Hwange cottage, we quivered as we felt the earth-tremor-shaking from the lions' roars. It was rivetingly powerful, and it became a part of our African DNA.

On this 2018 return trip back to Africa, I had watched powerful African lions copulating to insure the survival of the species. The privilege of that multi-sensory experience went way beyond the esoteric value: The continent used to be home to 200,000 lions. There are only 20,000 left. Man has decimated their numbers, and it would be an inconceivable travesty if these big wild cats were completely eradicated from their natural habitat by the end of this century.

There are so many life lessons that Africa has taught me: I've learned to be more sensitive to my surroundings - to listen, watch, and observe. Animals, particularly elephants, teach us how to be better human beings, and Africa has given me a valuable perspective of time on a larger scale.

Saying goodbye to the inviolable bonds I have with so many people there, and leaving behind the rich red earth, affects me profoundly. The flight home is interminably long, and the tears dry only with encroaching sleep. But as I touch down at Los Angeles International Airport, the golden nugget is always the massive reckoning of how fortunate I am to have such deeply entrenched relationships and passions across the world. For every tear, there is the corollary of a richly-spent life.

The USA has given me powerful roots in the second sunrise of my life. Just like the baobab tree, whose sense of physical safety impacted me so vividly in my childhood, my adoptive country feels like the immovable, massive trunk of a baobab tree that can weather any life storm. Its sturdy physical presence lends comfort to my genotype.

My seven-year-old perception of life being incredibly beautiful while also being so dangerously imperfect – has not changed. But a lifetime of experience has shown me that the goodness and grace alliance produces miracles from the worst of circumstances. My fervent hope is that through all my experiences, I can provide a compass to Téa and the young people in my life that I love deeply - so that they can navigate their boats in harmony with the oceans' currents – rather than beat up against them. Most importantly, I want them to pursue passionately well-spent lives in which their fires burn brilliantly.

Téa and Di, Cape Town 2018

Moore family- Brooke, Taylor, Sophia, Terry, Brenda

Giraffe, Marataba Safari Lodge - 2018

Marataba jeep - Di, Deborah and Noah - 2018

Final day Marataba Safari Lodge, Elephant swaying on 3 legs, 2018

2 young Lions - Marataba Safari Lodge 2018

Lion cub stares at us from behind a spider web while mom sleeps. Marataba 2018

Rhino pair - Marataba 2018

Last Safari night- Lion confrontation - Marataba Safari Lodge 2018

Night Safari Marataba, South Africa 2018 - Male Lion mating with Lioness

Marataba Lodge Bedrooms